Lessons from the Field:

Organizing in Rural Communities

Edited by Joe Szakos and Kristin Layng Szakos

Copyright © 2008 American Institute for Social Justice / Social Policy Magazine

All rights reserved. No part of this work may be reproduced or copied in any form or by any means – graphic, electronic, or mechanical – without the written permission of the publisher.

Edited by Joe Szakos and Kristin Layng Szakos with help from Valerie Coffin, Caitlin Corrigan and Rachel Norman.

Photos in the book were provided by Larry Yates, Ben Greenberg, Jerry Hardt, Kevin Dowling, Marcy Westerling, Laura Ramirez, Diana Bustamante, Steve Brooks, Erin Garvey, the Virginia Organizing Project and ACORN.

Cover design by Max Rivera

Manufactured in the United States of America
ISBN 13: 978-0-9799215-0-6

Social Policy Magazine
2609 Canal Street, 5th Floor • New Orleans, Louisiana 70119
1(800) 869-6605
info@socialpolicy.org
www.socialpolicy.org

Lessons from the Field: Organizing in Rural Communities

Table of Contents

Acknowledgments 5

Introduction 7
By Joe Szakos

Rural Organizing Project: An Evolving Struggle 15
By Mike Edera and Marcy Westerling

Who is Rural America? Opportunities and Considerations
for Rural Progressive Organizing 32
By Gary Sandusky

Up Close and Personal:
The Interpersonal Dynamics of Organizing in Rural America 42
By Gary Sandusky

Organizing in the Colonias of New Mexico – A Photo Essay 46
By Diana Bustamante

Rural Organizing in the Northern Great Plains
and Rocky Mountain West 52
By Margaret MacDonald

The Country Roads that Created ACORN 59
By Wade Rathke

The Evolution of a Leader: MacDonald Johnson 69
By Joe Szakos

Keys to Rural Organizing – Leadership Development 72
By Burt Lauderdale

A Conversation Between Leaders: Teri Blanton and Tayna Fogle 84
By Burt Lauderdale

Lessons in Rural Organizing 88
By Ellen Ryan

The Women's Leadership Network:
A New Approach to Community Organizing in Arkansas 97
By Lauren Hall

Organizing LGBT Folks in the Rural South 104
By Mandy Carter and Kristin Layng Szakos

Learning from Experience 107
By Steve Brooks

Why Organize Rural America? 115
By Allen Cooper

Endnotes 127

Acknowledgments

There are lots of great community organizers in rural areas throughout the United States and we want to take this opportunity to express our appreciation to all of them! Special thanks to a group of progressive rural organizers who met in the Washington, D.C., offices of the Center for Community Change in November 2005. They provided a lot of ideas for this book, especially for the Introduction. The group included Lisa Abbott, Carol Bishop, Diana Bustamante, Don Elmer, Mary Louise Frenchman, Daria Gere, LeeAnn Hall, Leonard Riley Jr., Gary Sandusky, Patrick Sweeney, Joe Szakos and Marcy Westerling.

People who were helpful in developing the project include Gayle Williams, Sandra Mikush, Dave Beckwith, William Dietel, Gary Sandusky, Cris Doby, Wade Rathke and Judy Matsuoka. Caitlin Corrigan and Valerie Coffin, managing editors at Social Policy, were terrific to work with.

Thanks, too, to the individuals and foundations who supported this project: the Mary Reynolds Babcock Foundation, Barbara Ehrenreich, the Dowager Fund of the Northern Piedmont Community Foundation, the Entelco Foundation, the Lived Theology Project at the University of Virginia, Agricultural Missions and the Center for Community Change.

We appreciate the reviewers who read drafts of the essays and offered helpful comments: David Barish, Allen Cooper, Steve Fisher, Bekah Menning, Andy Mott and Randy Stoecker.

We also want to thank our transcribers, Claire Jolly and Victoria Young. Bev Sell and Kathy Reese provided the idea for the cover; Max Rivera did the final design and was responsible for the format of the book. Joe Szakos, Kristin Layng Szakos, Larry Yates, Ben Greenberg, Jerry Hardt, Kevin Dowling, Marcy Westerling, Laura Ramirez, Diana Bustamante, Steve Brooks, Erin Garvey, the Virginia Organizing Project and ACORN provided photos.

And of course we want to recognize the thoughtful contributions of all the essayists: Steve Brooks, Mandy Carter, Allen Cooper, Lauren Hall, Burt Lauderdale, Margie MacDonald, Wade Rathke, Ellen Ryan, Gary Sandusky, Marcy Westerling and Mike Edera.

Introduction

By Joe Szakos

I can still remember the day in June 1984 when, as a young community organizer, I went to meet with Ed Chambers, head of the Industrial Areas Foundation, whose ten-day organizer training I was attending. IAF trains hundreds of new and aspiring organizers and its methods are used in groups from coast to coast. Ed greeted me warmly and then said, "Joe, why are you wasting your life in rural Kentucky?"

I had moved to Eastern Kentucky after organizing in Chicago for two years, convinced that rural areas couldn't be ignored if we wanted to see real progressive change nationwide. I had, in fact, sought out one of the least organized – and maybe one of the hardest to organize – parts of rural America to see if organizing there could make a real difference.

But it seemed like "rural" bothered Ed.

"Rural areas are important in this country," I told him, "and I don't know why everyone organizing for social change thinks they can ignore them. Our food, lumber for our houses, energy for heating and air conditioning, our recreation areas and water supplies and more – what goes on in rural areas affects us all."

Ed wasn't convinced.

"Take our national energy policy," I went on as he smiled politely at me. "Do you know that a majority of the members of the Senate committee that deals with national energy issues come from rural states with tiny populations?

"No," Ed conceded.

"Well, they do. And the senators who represent small rural states have a lot of other powerful leadership positions. If people in those states were organized and were putting pressure on their senators, it would make a real difference."

"OK," Ed said. "I just learned something today."

And then we had one of the best conversations about organizing strategy I have ever had. Ed stretched my thinking, especially about some constituencies who could be allies if we figured out what their self-interest was, instead of just making assumptions about what they thought. He also helped me learn ways to analyze power in Kentucky and how to incorporate evaluation into our work more effectively.

IAF still doesn't work in rural areas. All the major national organizing networks – ACORN, DART, Gamaliel, IAF and PICO — still concentrate their efforts on working with people who live in big and middle-sized cities. Few national organizations today work rurally and those that do are mostly limited to agricultural issues.

Even statewide groups in states that have large rural areas work as if there were just empty space between the urban centers — where all their organizing is concentrated.

Literature about organizing in rural areas is equally scant. With the notable

Introduction

exception of Paul Wellstone's *How the Rural Poor Got Power*, organizing manuals and theoretical books, from Saul Alinsky to the current struggles for a living wage, focus on organizing in the cities.

But there is some very good organizing for progressive social change going on in rural areas. As the essayists in this collection show, many rural states have effective citizens organizations that bring ordinary people together with extraordinary results. And so, in an effort to fill at least one space on organizing bookshelves with a work devoted to rural community organizing, we have asked a group of experienced organizers to share with us their experiences and the wisdom of their years working in rural and small town America. The result is the book you see here: *Lessons from the Field: Organizing in Rural Communities*.

Why rural community organizing is important

The strength of community-based organizing has long been understood by those in the conservative wing of American politics. The Moral Majority, the Christian Coalition, even the Republican Party, have used grassroots rural organizing to shift the balance of power in the country's heartland.

Throughout the 1990s, the Moral Majority and other groups worked to transform a political conservative Christians into a powerful force to support a right-wing political agenda. Through churches, radio programs and rural social networks, they mobilized their supporters to elect conservative school boards (boards that would introduce creationist curriculum and ban books that offered other perspectives), town councils (councils that would post the 10 Commandments on council chamber walls), state delegates (delegates who would pass laws to ban abortion or same-sex unions) and, ultimately, a president.

They found a kindred spirit in George W. Bush, who catered to the conservative evangelical vote through two elections. The work to get out the vote for Bush – both times – was done at the grassroots level and was done effectively in rural areas and small towns. As a result of those efforts, voters with a narrow understanding of George Bush's religious beliefs put and kept a man in office who did not represent their interests: a man who has increased unemployment, endangered the environment, created a huge deficit, weakened the dollar, planned to dismantle Social Security and sent the nation's sons and daughters to fight an unprovoked and disastrous war.

Those in the right wing knew – and some progressives have known all along – that there is power in rural communities. The cynical organizing of the right, though, has exploited this power for its own agenda, convincing rural folks to support policies that were not in their own best interests. Progressive organizing is different. True community organizing encourages people to work for positive change for the whole community, to reach solutions that benefit the largest number of people.

Rural areas, like urban areas, vary from place to place, depending on geography, culture, traditions, weather and the economy. But there are some obvious differences between rural organizing and urban organizing. Rural areas have more distance, fewer media outlets and less cell phone and Internet access.

Introduction

Rural areas have fewer libraries and bookstores, less job mobility and rarely are there alternative speaking venues. There are also fewer citizens groups to learn from in sparsely populated areas.

Research by Azzurra Cox (See, "Least populated states getting more power in the U.S. Senate") indicates that small "rural" states still have a lot of power.

Least populated states getting more power in the U.S. Senate
By Azzurra Cox

In order to generate a comprehensive analysis of the correlation between the least populated—and least organized—U.S. states and voice in the Senate, I researched state representation through membership in Senate Committees. These statistics are from both the 2001-02 term (107th Congress) and the 2005-06 term (109th Congress). During both terms, I found that a considerable percentage of Senate Committees was composed of fifty percent or more senators from the least populated states. In addition, even when the majority of certain Committee members did not represent those states, one or both of the senior members frequently did. Lastly, there was a marked increase in the Committee presence of the least populated states from 2001-02 to 2005-06, which seems to point to the general shift in the locus of power from the urban to the more rural areas of the United States.

During the 107th U.S. Congress, of the twenty Senate Committees, twenty-five percent of them were composed of fifty percent or more senators from the twenty least populated states.[1] Among those were the Committees on Agriculture, Nutrition, & Forestry; Appropriations; and Finance, which all carry significant weight in the making of American domestic policy. The least populated states were especially dominant in Indian Affairs and Select Ethics. Additionally, fifty-five percent of the Committees had one or both senior members (the positions of "Chairman" and "Ranking Member") representing the least populated states.

During the 109th Congress, of the twenty-one Senate Committees (change due to establishment of the Homeland Security & Governmental Affairs Committee), thirty-three percent are composed of fifty percent or more senators from the twenty least populated states. Among those are the Committees on Homeland Security; Appropriations; Commerce, Science, & Technology; and Finance. The least populated states were especially dominant in Indian Affairs, Select Ethics and Finance. A significant eighty-one percent of the Committees currently have one or both senior members from the least populated states.

These statistics represent the Congressional term immediately following the presidential elections and demonstrate how instrumental the presidential vote becomes in distributing power away from traditionally more influential urban settings. After the 2004 elections, one can see a significant rise in the representation of the least populated states in Senate Committees and that rise corresponds with the increase of red states representation. These statistics support the notion of the importance of grassroots mobilizing and organizing in the least populated states because it is clear that they, indeed, play a significant role in national politics. Incidentally, the two last presidential elections have also given less populated states — such as New Hampshire, New Mexico and West Virginia — a new importance as swing-states that are in a position to decide the entire electoral outcome. In those states, a concerted effort directed at organizing at the community level would have the potential to, in the long-run, affect policy on a national scale.

But what does rural community organizing really look like? The answers can be as different as the rural communities in which it is happening. But some

Introduction

key themes emerge when we take a good look at rural organizing. I met with a group of experienced rural organizers in November 2005 and we came up with the following themes about rural organizing, plus a list of challenges facing organizers today.

In rural areas, residents' shared sense of place creates a critical connection between them. The reason so many people remain in rural communities with declining economies is because place has such an important value in their lives. For many rural families, the connection to place is a deep part of their identity and this shared bond can be an important basis for organizing.

In many ways, organizers working in rural areas have more opportunity for access to people and to power than their counterparts in urban areas. Rural communities have small populations, so all relationships happen in closer proximity and can easily overlap. Rural residents and groups are more likely to have access to elected officials, since they may be neighbors or friends or perhaps relatives of people in the group. All relationships are a little more "up close and personal" than urbanites are generally accustomed to. The person you target for action this morning may be eating at the next table in the restaurant where you have lunch at noon.

This creates an atmosphere where "everything is accessible." Generally the work to get in the room with public decision-makers in rural areas is less than that required in urban areas. This access doesn't necessarily always translate into immediate influence, but it is an indicator of the ways that the rural organizing approach is different.

Ready access to public officials can also mean that organizing on an issue can move surprisingly quickly from local work into larger arenas — state, federal, or corporate power. Small communities have few resources and often have little decision-making authority over the key issues that affect people's lives.

But rural organizing can also move very slowly. The risks for active leaders in rural organizing can be high and very personal. The very people benefiting from injustice can be in the next pew at church on Sunday — so the risks of being a controversial figure in a rural community are very real. This tends to make active people thoughtful about the risks they take.

By the same token, the tactics we would endorse wholeheartedly in an urban area can be counterproductive in a rural community because it escalates the debate beyond what is useful. This is true in part because relationships are so accessible; people can take aggressive organizing tactics personally. Rural organizers and leaders learn to move through these limitations and advance the work anyway, but sometimes that takes more time.

Organizing work in rural areas can serve as a laboratory for organizing in general. Rural areas are on the forefront of solving some of the big organizing dilemmas. For instance, rural people wrestle directly with corporate power around natural resource exploitation that contaminates land and water and directly assaults the rural way of life. Every public issue on the national radar screen plays out in rural areas, from drug abuse to lack of access to health care, to energy costs, to immigration, to low-wage work issues and so on.

Finding the solutions to these issues that work for rural people will help

Introduction

frame and articulate progressive values in terms that are more likely to resonate on the national level. This is largely due to the fact that rural areas can be viewed as a microcosm of the national political mindset. Rural organizers cannot be as selective about who they relate to — cannot select only for constituencies that tow a progressive line. Rather, rural organizing must find the issue and political path that appeals to a broad segment of the rural population simply to get the numbers necessary to win.

There are fewer second chances to get it right when organizing in rural areas. This tends to move rural organizing to be a little more thoughtful and prepared when launching issues. Rural people tend to have long memories and tend to be less mobile, so the people rural organizers have to work with are the people who live there. It is not always possible to switch gears and go on to work with others — there aren't any others.

Rural people — in many ways — have more to lose if organizing proceeds badly.

All of these factors tend to move rural organizing toward long-term solutions to social, economic and environmental issues.

Rural organizers have other challenges facing them today. Among them are:

- Does there need to be a connection between community organizing and electoral work for a real shift in the balance of power?

- How "big" does community organizing have to be to really make a difference, not just to stop corruption or fight injustice, but to be proactive and make long-term changes?

- How can we attract and keep qualified staff and have adequate resources to do solid organizing?

- How can we create deliberate programs for intentional leadership development and personal growth, as well as internal political education workshops to get people to make connections between the many issues that they face?

- How can community organizing be effective at all levels — local, state and federal?

Hopefully, the essays in this collection will provide some insights into these questions.

Lots of great reading ahead

We asked the essayists for this collection to "download" some of their thoughts, to share some of the important lessons they have learned about community organizing in rural areas. Different experiences, different insights and different writing styles all contribute to a wonderful collection. Here's a quick tour through the book.

Mike Edera and Marcy Westerling write about using "values-based

Introduction

organizing to advance a progressive vision of democracy in Oregon" that has been used by the Rural Organizing Project since 1992. "We have restored hope to people who had almost given up believing in the power of the progressive social justice vision," they write. Edera and Westerling provide details of lessons they have learned since Oregon became a battleground in the "culture wars" in the early 1990s, when an "organized, conservative, Christian social movement seemed to emerge full-blown from nowhere to put an alternative worldview on the public agenda."

"Rural areas are not what you see on TV," Gary Sandusky tells us. "They are distinct and dynamic places with some major new demographic trends that create opportunities for progressive organizing." Sandusky warns us, though, "To take advantage of the available opportunities, however, organizing must cross boundaries of geography, culture, race and language. Doing that effectively demands the creation of multi-constituency organizations that develop internal clarity about how to respectfully accommodate differences and share leadership across these boundaries."

Margaret MacDonald shares some insights gained through the work of the Western Organization of Resource Councils over the past 35 years. One of the kernels she shares is that "Leadership in rural communities is not always obvious. Some of the most respected opinion leaders may stay quiet in public settings, but they are the ones that people listen to and respect. In developing and supporting leaders, it is important for organizers to recognize and seek out those quiet but respected voices."

Wade Rathke reminisces about his early days of ACORN — the Association of Community Organizations for Reform Now — and some reasons why ACORN decided to concentrate on urban areas. Rathke shares the lessons the group gained in rural Arkansas, South Dakota, Texas and Iowa. "We learned we could not live on the back roads if we were going to build a mass organization of low- and moderate-income families, but we learned how we could combine the urban core with the exurban folks just past the city line," Rathke writes.

Stressing the importance of leadership development in rural organizing, Burt Lauderdale writes, "True leadership helps us stay oriented toward a long-term goal even as we strive mightily for short-term victories. It keeps the best interests of all of us in the forefront of decision-making, while encouraging emerging voices to speak to their self-interest. Great grassroots community leadership breaks the stereotypes of leaders as technically expert, elite, powerful, wealthy individuals. It gives us other models and holds out the best opportunity for preserving and evolving our democracy."

"The very best community organizing is about building power to create positive change, but it is also about building that power with integrity and in service of the shared interest of all of us," Lauderdale writes. "Giving of yourself for the benefit of your community is the essential motivation and the distinguishing quality of the most effective, more productive, most inspiring grassroots community leaders. And the most effective leadership development practices expect, foster, reward and reproduce this type of inspired and inspiring community leadership."

Introduction

Ellen Ryan has worked in more than fifteen states since starting her organizing career in 1973. "The role that organizing plays in engaging people in active participation in public life nourishes and sustains democracy in ways that can't be replaced by other institutions such as education or the media alone," she writes. "This is because organizing creates voluntary associations of people who work together to get things done in the public arena."

"Rural people may speak more slowly on average than people in cities," Ryan writes. "But taking time to think before one speaks and to listen to what others have to say is a cultural practice worth spreading. Deliberate community organizing, rather than just signing people on to campaigns, also provides an opportunity to challenge cultural practices that aren't fair."

Lauren Hall interviewed four women associated with the Women's Leadership Network (WLN) in Arkansas. The WLN has two goals: (1) to work with women in their communities to make them more effective leaders and (2) to help break the barrier of isolation that rural women face and bring them together to share their skills, their resources and also their struggles. Observing a monthly gathering of women in the network, Hall writes, "I begin to see the state of Arkansas as a web of strings threaded through the center of the state, each reaching out to the corners and across the rivers and onto places on the map where roads are not marked. Technology plays an important role in this network, but the WLN looks to the relationships to embolden the array. These mean everything."

Mandy Carter shares some lessons about getting the lesbian, gay, bisexual and transgendered community active in rural areas in the South. For example, Carter says, "What we found out, especially with lesbians, is that they have their own networks in rural parts of North Carolina. And the way they would get their work done, if I can use that term, the way they would coordinate organizing would be through a potluck or some kind of informal social event at someone's home."

Writing about his personal journey of rural organizing, Steve Brooks says that a key lesson is that "though organizing tools have changed over the years, especially with computers and email, it still takes personal contact to make things happen."

Allen Cooper gives some historical perspective when he explores the influence of Thomas Jefferson on our country's history and why Jefferson believed rural areas were so important: "Jefferson thought rural America was important to democracy in the nation as a whole because the agrarian life offered economic independence. But today, rural communities often suffer from the worst sort of economic dependence, serving in a colonial capacity as natural resource reservoirs to the national economy. High rates of unemployment and poverty often result. As Jefferson predicted, one result of economic dependency among citizens is that dominant economic interests often capture state political institutions because they can channel money to political campaigns and bring an extraordinary level of resources to bear in a policy dispute. This is one reason why rural communities are unattractive to organize today: even if the people are organized, their power is minor relative to the national or multinational corporations that dominate the state's economy and politics. But that is precisely the reason why it is important to organize a rural state: the nation as a whole suffers if a rural state is captive to the interests of an economically powerful group, because that group's hold on a state gives it disproportionate influence in national elections and policy controversy."

Also included in this collection about rural community organizing is a photo essay of organizing in the Colonias in New Mexico by Diana Bustamante and leadership stories of MacDonald Johnson, Teri Blanton and Tayna Fogle.

We hope that you will find these essays full of inspiration and information – and that they will offer some tools for the expansion of rural organizing across the country.

Rural Organizing Project: An Evolving Struggle

By Mike Edera and Marcy Westerling

According to conventional wisdom, the Left fails to talk values with voters, particularly voters in rural (now "red") communities. Beneath this popular story line is a more complex reality. Rural voters care about values, yes – but those values are not necessarily conservative. For over twelve years, the Rural Organizing Project has used values-based organizing to advance a progressive vision of democracy in Oregon, the tenth-largest state in the country, where all thirty-six counties have a rural profile.

Roots of reaction

In the early 1990s, Oregon became a battleground in the "culture wars." An organized, conservative, Christian social movement seemed to emerge full-blown from nowhere to put an alternative worldview on the public agenda. In 1992, the conservative Oregon Citizens Alliance launched a statewide constitutional ballot measure to define homosexuality as "abnormal and perverse" and to forbid state agencies from doing anything perceived to "promote the homosexual agenda." To most Oregonians, it's safe to say this political thrust appeared like a bizarre bolt out of the blue. But the religious right-wing movement had been developing under the radar for over a decade in a state known to the rest of the nation as a model of forward-looking progressive policies. The political base of this new conservative insurgency was rural Oregon.

It was no accident that rural Oregon had turned sharply to the right by 1992. Beginning in the late 1970s, the rural economy entered a tailspin from which it has not emerged to this day. The national recession of the early 1980s was a depression in timber-dependent communities. Tens of thousands of high-paying union jobs disappeared as lumber and paper mills closed and logging operations shut down. Small businesses went bankrupt and Main Streets began to atrophy. The timber economy had supported a prosperous small-town lifestyle since the end of World War II. The crash was caused by over-logging and long-term timber industry plans to replace older Pacific Northwest timber stands with newer forests in the southeastern United States. The economic pain in rural Oregon was neither adequately explained to the victims nor dealt with effectively by industry and government. Instead, convenient scapegoats stepped right onto the stage in the late 1980s when environmentalists filed lawsuits to halt old-growth logging.

Environmental lawsuits to protect the last stands of ancient forest and defend endangered species like the spotted owl were, in truth, efforts to preserve the ecologically sensitive remains of the national forests. But to out-of-work loggers and mill workers watching the rest of the state and nation enjoy economic expansion while they remained stuck, the environmental organizations seemed like malicious interlopers. The first reaction was the formation of a coalition of timber corporations, chambers of commerce, conservative politicians and unions that organized log truck convoys and rallies to protest environmentalist meddling and federal court rulings to protect the spotted owl. This coalition was portrayed as made up of city-based, latte-drinking elitists who preferred animals and bugs to people. The pro-timber, anti-forest-protection movement was a rapid groundswell, but it was not able to restore the timber economy, whose real-world, material base had been destroyed by corporate forces beyond local control.

The character of rural and small-town Oregon was changing radically. The years of timber prosperity had generated a live-and-let-live social culture that was the base of Oregon's nationally famous moderate progressive political reputation, exemplified by liberal Republicans such as former Governor Tom McCall, Senator Mark Hatfield and pro-choice Republican Bob Packwood. On the ground, the Main Street leadership was also essentially moderate, pro-government and pro-environment. In the late 1960s and 1970s, rural Oregon accepted an influx of countercultural newcomers: organic gardeners, craftspeople and builders and later in the decade, telecommuting professionals. But when the economy crashed, the social fault lines were exposed.

Alongside (and in reaction to) the countercultural changes of the 1970s, another alternative culture had developed with the growth of fundamentalist religious communities. Hard-hit timber workers and small business owners, whose own anti-environmentalist movement was going nowhere, entered the orbit of the new, growing "non-denominational" churches that offered a combination of a caring community on a personal level with a paranoid political worldview. The movement identified forces such as feminism, gay liberation and liberalism as the causes behind the social stresses that economically strapped families were experiencing. These were "molecular changes," happening beneath the radar of conventional, business-as-usual politics. Eventually, this socially conservative grassroots movement linked up with national institutions of the so-called New Right. The subsequent launch of politically sophisticated campaigns in favor of primitive social goals took both the political establishment and the progressive movement by surprise.

Progressive response – Columbia County Citizens

Before we knew that the growth of a reactionary right was a national phenomenon, progressive rural Oregonians did know that our communities were under siege. Awareness grew in the late 1980s and early 1990s as people watched hiccups of small town conservatism erupt into harsh community divisions. Books were censored with increased regularity. The merits of teaching creationism were debated at seven-hour school board meetings. Anti-gay policies were on the ballot again and again, in both statewide and local initiatives. Many fair-minded people did not have the words to describe what was happening in their towns, but they knew there was an escalating trend that had everyone on edge. One bizarre sign of the times that came during a heated anti-gay ballot measure was the appearance of eight-by-eleven-inch placards in car windows portraying two male silhouettes engaged in anal sex, with the international stop slash through the image. These same cars boasted bumper stickers supporting family values. There was little room for dialogue.

To cope, progressive residents of small towns started congregating. This led to the organizing of human rights groups. It was an organic response at which many small-town progressives arrived simultaneously; we needed progressive infrastructure in order to push back.

The story of the formation of one "human dignity group" illustrates a process that was replicated across the state. In the early 1990s, Columbia County, in the northwest corner of Oregon, was home to 37,000 people, seven small towns, the state's only nuclear reactor (soon to be defunct) and a shrinking paper and timber industry. It was characterized by unemployment at more than ten percent and rising and a growing struggle over who would define the community: right-wing Christians and other organized bigots or those who believed in democracy for all. Like other rural parts of the Northwest, Columbia County seemed an ideal haven for Christian warriors who hoped to turn the clock back to a time before the great social justice movements of the Twentieth Century.

At the same time, many others in Columbia County had watched the growth of the right wing with alarm from our silent corners of the community. Occasionally we gathered, but even then we assembled as individuals rather than as members of an organized response. At the end of any given meeting we each went home in despair, feeling as if we were losing control of our community – and we were.

In August of 1991, a hopeful development occurred. A small group of community leaders and everyday citizens (often one and the same) met over a potluck supper to name what was happening to our community. As was true elsewhere in the state, the impetus came from the local feminist rape and domestic violence prevention program, the Columbia County Women's Resource Center (CCWRC). With its long history in the community of opposing

oppression-based violence, challenging dominant social norms and organizing among targeted groups, the CCWRC was able to provide clear analysis of the present danger and the need to develop counter-strategies.

The most immediate cause for alarm was a campaign to amend the Oregon constitution to require discrimination on the basis of sexual orientation. Passage of the initiative would have marked the first time a state constitution had been amended to take away the rights of a group of people. People in Columbia County were concerned about the implications – we were not ready to allow democracy to be so weakened.

For the first time, we talked about what each of us saw: homophobia, social control, Christian authoritarianism and disinformation. We all shared our clear commitment to reclaim our community as a place that did not tolerate bigotry, as a place that actively protected the minority voice – a community committed to democracy. The power of this initial meeting gave us tremendous energy to move forward together into action.

Our immediate strategy was to gather a strong base of support. Our strength would come not only from sheer numbers but also from the diversity that would truly represent our community. We took on the task of meeting with neighbors, co-workers, family members and friends who had a history of leadership and ethics. Such criteria led us to approach fundamentalist Christians, loggers and other individuals not traditionally seen as aligned with the progressive community. The common ground was the concern over erosion of civil rights and the immediate targeting of the gay and lesbian community. Soon our base of support included people of color, Christians, pagans, Jews, laborers, office workers, a few gays and lesbians and a lot of committed heterosexuals.

We talked with people about what we were seeing and presented them with the hopeful prospect that a group was organizing to unite our voices. Most people we approached asked to join the project and also sought out a role for themselves. We found it critical to have some ready tasks for each new member, even if the task was as simple as approaching five others. None of us could remember a time where people were so ready to move into action.

Once we had a base of support of almost fifty people clearly signed on to reclaim our community, we felt we had a credible and safe starting point for formalizing our group. We drafted a mission statement. This was an invaluable tool as we set out to attract additional folks. We struggled to come up with a name that would represent our group perfectly and compromised on a name that offended none in our group. We acquired papers from the county clerk to establish Columbia County Citizens for Human Dignity as an official organization, which enabled us to raise the money we knew we would need. We elected officers. By then, we were learning how to work with one another. Once we elected our official steering committee, designed our letterhead and agreed upon our decision-making process, we were truly ready to move outward into our community.

Selecting an initial strategy for outreach with the community was hard. By then we had encountered the Oregon Citizens Alliance, the religious right-wing group seeking to place the anti-gay Measure 9 on the ballot through the public initiative process. We had peacefully attended a few of their meetings and observed them taking over the supermarket and post office in one of our towns to gather signatures for the ballot measure. It hurt and almost immobilized us to witness our neighbors advancing bigotry. Our initial response was confusion: for a week we struggled to find a direction for action. Again, our high standards slowed us down as we sought the "perfect" strategy. It took a few discussions before we recognized that moving forward with plans that were ethically sound was more realistic than waiting for the perfect campaign plan.

We finally took some simple steps. We designed a signature form to gather the names of friends and neighbors who would publicly affiliate themselves with us in future education efforts. More immediately, the signature form served as a tool to start discussions. We sent a press release announcing our formation to our local papers. We compiled one hundred "organizer's packets" that described what our group was about and provided tips on how to move into action. Small-group discussions were set up with potential allies, providing each participant with accurate information and an opportunity to sign on to the campaign. We began to attend local candidate forums to ask where each candidate stood on civil rights. We moved down the roster of churches and community groups and met with them one by one. The local papers printed editorials, articles and letters reflecting our views and activities.

Throughout all these projects we kept our meetings minimal and fun. Food and casual settings were incorporated. Whenever possible, we tried to anticipate potential barriers to participation; we found rides for those without cars and made sure children were included in meetings.

Largely because of efforts like ours, Measure 9 was defeated, but the right-wing forces continued to work to erode human rights in Oregon.

Thirteen years later, Columbia County Citizens is still a work in progress. We interweave our strategies into our everyday lives in the community. Our most effective strategies are very simple. Most accomplish the immediate task of breaking down the isolation of rural progressive people and broadening our campaign to provide information to our decent, often conservative neighbors who have rarely been asked to challenge their perceptions. By demonstrating our diversity and strength in numbers, we inspire many to take their first public stands for social justice and to re-commit others who had long ago given up hope and action. Again and again, we've found that a decade of repressive politics has made many people eager to grab hold of the opportunity to belong to a group that stands for human dignity. We have restored hope to people who had almost given up believing in the power of the progressive social justice vision.

The Rural Organizing Project

The same process of reaction and response in Columbia County from 1991 to 1993 was taking place across rural Oregon and for the same reasons. Throughout the region, the Christian right was mobilizing – behind the OCA's statewide ballot measure, campaigns for local anti-gay ordinances and right-wing primary election challengers to moderate Republican state legislators. And wherever these conservative challenges emerged, local progressives responded by creating

human rights and human dignity groups.

The people who joined human dignity groups fit into certain categories. A significant percentage was self-employed, often in newer information industries, crafts, as well as more traditional trades. Many folks cobbled together several employment sources. Another large percentage was employed in "caring professions," such as teaching and in social services. People tended to be middle-income, with at least some college education, who were confronting the economic problems of the middle class in a depressed rural economy.

Despite the dramatic ease with which groups like Columbia County Citizens formed, it was clear that rural progressives were up against powerful, divisive opponents, with only a limited progressive infrastructure at their back. It was critical that we craft an organization run by and for rural progressives to provide ongoing behind-the-scenes support to rural groups. Such an organization could ensure that triumphs were shared during boom times and collapse was avoided during inevitable periods of economic ebbing.

The timing was right. Folks in community after community were concluding that traditional liberal politics run from the cities would not work in these new times. The leaders of the conservative culture war had declared that rural America was their constituency. For rural voters to navigate the hot-button wedge issues of God, gays and guns, of immigration and collapsing safety nets, their progressive neighbors were best positioned to develop the language of compassionate communication. A support system was vital if this was to happen.

Because of the national attention that Oregon attracted around the OCA's anti-gay campaigns, our developing network was able to make connections that were critical to the emerging vision for a rural progressive organization. Sponsored by the Oregon Coalition Against Domestic and Sexual Violence, Susanne Pharr in 1992 came to Oregon from the Women's Project in Arkansas to help create resistance to the right-wing mobilization. Working together, we combined consciousness-raising from the women's movement with the multi-issue, anti-racist approach of the Women's Project's anti-poverty work and put it on the road in rural Oregon.

Setting up meetings in the rural communities that had fought battles around OCA's local anti-gay campaigns, we brought people together to share experiences and discuss strategy. Scott Nakagawa of the Coalition for Human Dignity helped us with an analysis of the national and international structure of the right-wing movement and the links between Christian social conservatives and the racist right. We discovered that groups that experienced this type of consciousness-raising process were far better able to engage in long-term organizing than groups that rose up around a particular crisis or outrage without the benefit of seeing the big picture.

In 1993, we held the first Rural Caucus and Strategy Session, bringing together activists from each human dignity group around the state. At this session we decided to create a permanent statewide organization, the Rural Organizing Project (ROP), consisting of a network of more than forty human dignity groups, with a permanent staff to facilitate local organizing, communication and political analysis. Voting membership in the organization was relegated entirely to local, autonomous human dignity groups and board members were required to live in rural areas.

The Rural Organizing Project was created to allow local activists to control the terms of our own activism. We formed around some fairly basic notions: that every person mattered, that every issue was interconnected and that transformation needed to be the goal. We took our scarce resources (a budget of $18,000 in the first year and yet to exceed $200,000 per year) and created a different type of organization – one that valued being lean and mean, saw the value of local autonomy and measured success in the number of people to whom we reached out.

The local human dignity group proved to be an enduring form for local organizing. Meeting in living rooms, church basements and libraries, people came together to support each other and to do basic political activism such as writing letters, planning educational events and performing community canvasses. When concerned people meet face to face on a regular basis, this opens space for neighbors to break their isolation and take concrete, small steps to further social justice.

The ROP developed an analysis model that merged consciousness-raising about oppression with broader political education. This helped groups understand the wedge issues used by the right wing to divide communities. We tried to reframe issues in terms of a real, functioning democracy. We used a four-point definition of democracy from the World Book Encyclopedia, affirming that a true democracy requires majority rule, minority rights, an informed and educated public and an adequate standard of living. From this, we created a democracy grid that allowed people to judge any political initiative against the tenets of democracy.

The ROP helped each group use external projects to build internal capacity. We focused on ensuring that each group had a functional leadership team, a regularly utilized communication system and an action plan with that took into

DEMOCRACY TALKING POINTS
Connecting Democracy and Human Dignity Issues

1) Inclusion of all; Equality for all.

"Democracies have various arrangements to prevent any person or branch of government from becoming too powerful." "Throughout history, the most important aspects of the democratic way of life have been the principles of individual equality and freedom." (All quotes are from *The World Book Encyclopedia 1994* except where noted.)

In his State of the Union speech in 1941, a time when Hitler was sweeping across Europe, Franklin Roosevelt discussed four essential human freedoms. The first was freedom of speech and expression; the second was freedom of religious expression; the third was freedom from want; and the fourth was freedom from fear.

Roosevelt's freedom of speech and expression and freedom from fear seems especially pertinent to this principle of democracy. Only with freedom from fear and with freedom of speech and expression will all voices be heard.

What is meant by inclusion of all has changed over time as seen in the struggle for increased suffrage for those groups not originally included by our founding fathers. And genuine inclusion of all in a broader sense than voting rights is still not a reality. However, inclusion of all is an incredibly important goal of democracy. Based on ROP bylaws, inclusion of all includes age, color, economic status, education, marital status, national origin, parenthood, familial status, race, religion, gender, sexual identity or physical handicap.

2) Majority rule and minority rights.

"Majority rule is based on the idea that if all citizens are equal, the judgment of the many will be better than the judgment of a few." "Democratic countries guarantee that certain rights can never be taken from the people, even by extremely large majorities." "Most constitutions have a detailed bill of rights that describes the basic liberties of the people and forbids the government to violate those rights."

3) Democracy requires well-educated and well-informed people who participate in the democratic process.

"Democracy calls for widespread participation in politics by the people." "The quality of government depends on the quality of participation. Well-informed and well-educated citizens are able to participate more intelligently."

This principle requires that people move far beyond the "sound bite" level in their discussion and analysis of issues. This means research and digging up facts as well as careful analysis and open discussion of concerns. Applying this principle to anti-affirmative action efforts, for example, helps broaden that discussion to the underlying issue of racism and people's fears about economic decline that requires scapegoats rather than close examination of the widening gap between the haves and the have nots and how that gap is facilitated (or not) by government policies and business practices.

4) A reasonable standard of living – Economic justice.

"Most successful democracies have existed in developed societies. In such societies, literacy rates are high, per capita (per person) incomes are moderate to high and there are few extremes of wealth and poverty."

In his 1941 State of the Union speech, Roosevelt said, "Certainly this is no time for any of us to stop thinking about the social and economic problems which are the root cause of the social revolution which is today a supreme factor in the world. For there is nothing mysterious about the foundations of a healthy and strong democracy. The basic things expected by our people of their political and economic systems are simple. They are: Equality of opportunity for youth and for others. Jobs for those who can work. Security for those who need it." (From: *The American Reader*, editor, Diane Ravitch, Harper-Collins, 1990).

*Rural Organizing Project * POB 1350 Scappoose, OR 97056 * 503 543-8417 * www.rop.org*

Democracy Worksheet

Principals Issues	#1 Inclusion of All	#2 Majority rule, minority rights	#3 Well-informed and educated	#4 Reasonable standard of living

Rural Organizing Project – Advancing democracy in rural Oregon
PO Box 1350 • Scappoose, OR 97056 • (503) 543-8417 • www.rop.org

account issues of race, class and gender. Since the ROP was working with more than fifty groups at any one moment, we relied on a combination of constant traveling meetings to create organizational work plans and regular, standardized check-ins via phone and email. Every group could count on contacts from the office that combined cheerleading for successes along with honest nagging as we reviewed what might have fallen off the organizational to-do list.

Allies

In 1995, Oregon's farmworker union, Pineros y Campesinos Unidos del Noroeste (PCUN), called for a ten-year anniversary strawberry harvest job action to win improved wages and job conditions for Oregon's farmworkers. The ROP was able to mobilize support from human dignity groups throughout the region, which took shifts on the picket lines, provided logistical support and created favorable local public opinion in support of the job action. Three years earlier, PCUN had provided highly visible solidarity to the gay and lesbian community in the struggle against Measure 9, helping to blunt the right-wing attempt to drive a wedge between the embattled communities. The strawberry actions were an opportunity to repay a debt and cement an alliance. Later in the year, the ROP worked with CAUSA, the newly-formed immigrants' rights group, to derail an attempt to float anti-immigrant ballot measures modeled on California's infamous Proposition 187 of 1994.

Over the years the ROP has continued to work with CAUSA and PCUN. Together, we resisted the Immigration and Naturalization Services' brutal immigrant busts in 1997. We worked together again four years later to derail a plan by Oregon's United States Senators, Republican Gordon Smith and Democrat Ron Wyden, for a "guest-worker program" based on the infamous bracero program of the 1940s, which would have created a sub-class of immigrant workers at the complete mercy of their employers. The groups have worked together at every legislative session to oppose anti-immigrant and anti-worker legislation, defend the increased minimum wage and fight for the social safety net.

The human dignity groups have been able to "get" the need to work with the Latino community through interaction with principled, militant groups like PCUN and CAUSA. From the beginning, we tried to raise consciousness about race, gender and class issues, exposing the roots of social conservatism in racist movements like the 1968 George Wallace presidential campaign and pointing out the ways that the political base built around anti-gay and anti-abortion movements has been used to advance anti-union policies and efforts to wreck the social safety net. But there is no doubt that considering the circumstances under which the ROP was formed – in struggle against discriminatory legislation that targeted gay and lesbians – provided the shock that allowed people with white privilege to experience a little bit of what communities of color have undergone for generations.

An evolving struggle

The ROP was created in a moment of crisis, in the face of an insurgent right-wing movement which has changed in the last thirteen years. While particular statewide anti-gay initiatives were defeated at the polls and in-your-face organizations like the Oregon Citizens Alliance lost credibility, a powerful conservative political base was created through these battles and the more strategic leaders of the movement used this new political power to transform the Oregon Republican Party. From 1994 through today, the Right has targeted virtually every moderate Republican in the state Legislature, taking advantage of low voter turnout in primaries to install hard-right conservatives in Republican rural districts. Social conservatives have forged common cause with anti-tax activists, promoting a phony anti-government populism that has captured the economic anger in districts that have experienced over two decades of recession.

For its part, the ROP's network maintained itself and grew over this period and has continually sought to evolve a political program around the values of democracy and inclusion for all. As the battle with the Right shifted to the economic sphere, the ROP tried to fit issues such as tax justice and the need for social programs into its values-based language.

But the ROP is a minority within the liberal and progressive movement and that movement, by and large, has been hesitant, fearful, slow-footed and defensive in fighting the conservative assault on social programs. Consequently, the progressive Oregon of the early 1970s has lost every economic battle to conservative forces, unable to counter fake right-wing populism with an effective reply. Conservatives moved into the power position. Statewide offices in Oregon continue to be held by moderate Democrats, reflecting the weight of urban areas, but the Legislature has remained, until recently, under the complete control of the most conservative Republican Party in state history. Combining that position with the success of anti-tax ballot measures, conservatives managed to erode the tax base, shift the tax burden from corporations to individuals and continue to parley the economic anger of the lower middle class into political decisions

that make the situation worse for the middle class and better and better for the wealthy and big business.

This was the situation in Oregon on September 10, 2001 – conservatives wielding the initiative, with liberals retreating step by step, winning individual fights and losing the overall battle as Oregon changed from an innovative social laboratory to a backsliding retrograde state with the highest rate of poverty and the shortest school year in the nation.

Post-9/11 – a progressive insurgency?

The election of George W. Bush, the 9/11 attacks, the plunge into war in Afghanistan and Iraq – these events have changed the Oregon political landscape, as they have across the nation. The insurgent conservative movement of the early 1990s is firmly in power. They are the new establishment. The Democratic leadership in Oregon has continued its timorous routine of whistling past the graveyard, pining for a long-dead nirvana of bipartisanship. But at the grassroots level, progressives and moderate liberals have made common cause and mobilized into a new insurgency. The shocks of the last few years created wide mood swings in the public: a herding together behind the President in the wake of 9/11 and a continual erosion of that consensus as the administration's blatant lying and contempt for human rights became clear at least to half the population.

By 2003, Oregon saw some of the largest demonstrations against the war in Iraq in the nation, with tens of thousands marching week after week in Portland. Across rural Oregon, anti-war activities surfaced in small communities that had never witnessed protest from the left. A rolling demonstration went up and down the Oregon coast, with ROP-related activists gathering in different towns each week. Cowboy towns like Burns, Pendleton, Baker and The Dalles saw anti-war actions, organized primarily through the ROP network. A number of human dignity groups launched efforts to pass local ordinances opposing the USA Patriot Act. Human dignity group meetings across the state reported greatly increased attendance.

Election 2004

In 2004, the overwhelming sentiment in human dignity groups was to pull out the stops to kick Bush out. Many ROP activists, particularly those newer to the movement, advocated working entirely through the Democratic Party and local Democratic committees were strengthened throughout rural Oregon, especially in communities in which the Party had almost ceased to exist.

Some long-time ROP activists called for a different approach this time. Was there a way, we wondered, to build up local groups through electoral work, regardless of the election's outcome? Over the first three months of 2004, we held community meetings across the state. Out of these discussions came a new three-stage strategy.

In the first stage, local groups held house parties to involve as many people in election activism as possible. People were invited to talk about their hopes and fears for the elections and to commit to engaging in at least three election activities over the year.

As local groups built up their volunteer base, they moved into the next stage: a community conversation about the issues. People went door-to-door in selected precincts in their towns, asking folks to talk about the issues with which they were most concerned. Activists used a survey that we created to "frame" hot-button issues. Was there a way to express issues such as tax fairness, health care, same-sex marriage, the war in Iraq, or the Patriot Act in a way that would increase support for a progressive stand?

The third stage was a get-out-the-vote effort. People we surveyed were classified into three groups: those who responded to all our questions with a progressive disposition; swing voters, people who had opinions on both sides of the ideological divide (for example, we found many people who strongly opposed both the war in Iraq and gay marriage); and lastly, the ideological conservatives. We tried to follow up initial contact with the progressives and swing people with thank-you notes and pledge forms asking them to vote for fairness, democracy and equal rights. Finally, we distributed more than forty thousand voter guides that discussed some of the issues at stake in the election and publicized our positions on Oregon's numerous ballot measures, including Measure 36, which sought to ban same-sex marriage.

Seven ROP human dignity groups signed up to fulfill all three stages of our election strategy. Individual groups set their own goals for the number of people to contact. Local activists edited the survey until it became simple and clear enough for volunteers to use comfortably. Other groups around the state helped implement pieces of the election strategy as their own time and focus permitted. In all, more than five hundred volunteers participated. Some 3,300 people were surveyed. Over eight hundred new progressives were identified from the door-to-door work. ROP created individual databases for each group that conducted the surveys and conversations so that local groups could remain in contact with the people they had met on the doorsteps. The following pie charts show how people responded to our questions. Most of the surveys were done at random within a given precinct, with activists going to every door on the street.

The 2004 election strategy absorbed a great deal of energy within the ROP network and also created internal stresses. As the elections drew closer, many ROP activists whose primary commitments were to Democratic politics became very uncomfortable with an election strategy that did not directly work for specific election results. People who were terrified by the prospect of Bush's prospective re-election were often unable to think long-term, or to visualize a path that would build power beyond the election, even in the face of the eventual Bush victory.

We also did not anticipate how time-consuming the actual survey work would be. This phase was projected to end in July, but we didn't complete it until September, at which point local campaigns were clamoring for volunteers. We needed to cut short our get-out-the-vote efforts to free up people for more partisan campaign work. Since this was an experimental effort, we did not know what aspect would be the most important. We originally thought of the work as

Results From ROP's 2004 Community Survey

Noted Harvard Ethnographist Lynn Stephens reviewed ROP's work with rural and small town voters in the 2004 elections and said, "The results from 3,347 surveys are quite significant. It is a large sample and demonstrates a very important trend - that people vote differently than how they articulate their values in a conversation. The results indicate a much stronger progressive base to build on than voter returns would indicate. This is crucial information.

If we know how to frame the message of progressive politics in terms that people identify with and understand, then we can do a much better job in mobilizing them so that their votes match their values.

The right-wing spends lots of money and time contracting experts to conduct research like yours. They call it polling and marketing research. You are on the right track and uncovered important trends. I hope that ROP activists can appreciate the importance of this data and the strong indication it suggests for future organizing directions."

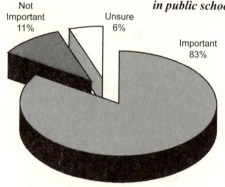

How important is it to make classes in public schools smaller?
Not Important 11%
Unsure 6%
Important 83%

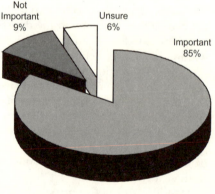

How important is it to close tax loopholes that let corporations avoid paying taxes?
Not Important 9%
Unsure 6%
Important 85%

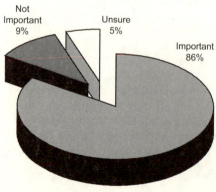

How important is it to help workers who've been laid off to retrain or start small businesses?
Not Important 9%
Unsure 5%
Important 86%

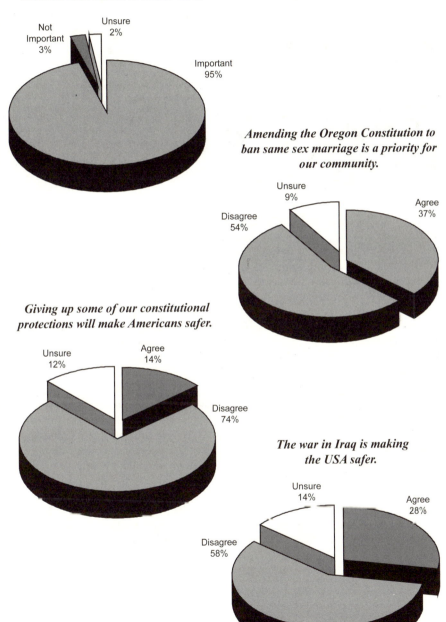

Results From ROP's 2004 Community Survey

a better way to engage voters to support progressive candidates and issues. As it turned out, the issue framing we did was the most significant result in terms of future direction.

The work to bring in new voters around a progressive platform will take considerably more time than one election cycle afforded. To really succeed in changing the political dynamic, ROP human dignity groups must be permanent fixtures in communities, using systematic tools like the survey to engage actively with people about the issues whether or not an election is afoot. We will need to struggle within our own base, encouraging our own activists to see beyond the next electoral emergency and to challenge the party structure to address the real issues rather than seeking the lowest common denominator and avoiding hard topics.

Bush's re-election indicated that the struggle to change America would require much deeper transformation with which power brokers within establishments such as the Democratic Party are uncomfortable. Courting the middle-of-the-road swing voter still did not provide the votes to topple the entrenched ideological right wing. The ROP's twelve-year experience in the belly of conservative rural Oregon suggests that people will step up to an unapologetically progressive message if it is expressed in everyday, inclusive language. We know now that social-change activists live even in the most "backwoods" communities and that the long history of American rural radicalism lives on today, in a different form. Given the famous red state/blue state map of our political division, a rural progressive movement will be the keystone of a new political alignment.

Rural Organizing Project: An Evolving Struggle

Marcy Westerling, *founder and director of the Rural Organizing Project (ROP), is a leader in organizing, educating and mobilizing rural communities. Her organizing background includes urban activism with ACORN, rural organizing through the battered women's movement and work with the developmentally disabled. ROP started in 1992, partially in response to Westerling's need to give voice to progressive values in her own small-town community. Westerling has called the small town of Scappoose her home for the last twenty-three years.*

Mike Edera *is a landscaper by day and a community organizer for the rest of his hours in the week. His multi-decade commitment to global justice combines his passion for understanding social justice in an historical context with his commitment to local action in small-town Oregon. He first became aware of the Rural Organizing Project in the early 1990s and he has provided active leadership ever since.*

Who is Rural America? Opportunities and Considerations for Rural Progressive Organizing

By Gary Sandusky

What is the "rural" in rural organizing?

There are lots of myths to debunk about rural organizing. The first starts with the term "rural" itself. Even the federal government has trouble defining the word and its definitions are based primarily on population and jurisdiction. For instance: the United States Department of Agriculture sometimes defines rural communities as places with fewer than 25,000 people. Yet the department often allows federal rural development funds to be used within areas that everyone knows will be annexed by larger jurisdictions very soon. The United States Department of Housing and Urban Development uses a population of 50,000 or more as its threshold to determine which cities are large enough to manage Community Development Block Grant funds. So what would we call a city with a population of between 25,000 and 50,000 people?

For most Americans, "rural" seems to be defined as "anything that isn't urban." And along with that definition come all kinds of stereotypes that are perpetuated by the entertainment industry.

Who is Rural America? Opportunities and Considerations for Rural Progressive Organizing

I often use the following set of phrases to help people see their own set of biases:

Rural is a place where...

MYTH (Stereotype)	REALITY
The bumpkin myth: Country folks have simple interests and are generally unsophisticated.	Many primarily rural states have higher high school graduation rates than their urban counterparts and meet or exceed national college graduation rates.
The back-to-the-land myth: Most people make their living off the land in the farming, timber and mining industries and life is simpler than in the city.	Of all North Dakota farms, 38 percent earned less than $10,000 in 2002. For the most part, small family farms are sustained by family members working at jobs off the farm. Only 10 percent of North Dakota farmers live on the land they farm. Simple living is largely a myth.
The "Green Acres" myth: Everybody knows your name and things stay the same.	The average age of a North Dakota farmer is 54 as the population ages and youth migrate elsewhere. The state continues to experience outright loss of population, losing 1.3 percent from 2001-2003.
The racial homogeneity myth: Everybody is white, except in the South.	Communities of color are growing in every state and they are influencing the politics. Native American and Latino people had the largest percentage growth in population in South Dakota from 1990-2000.
The "Andy Griffith Show" myth: Drugs and drug culture have yet to penetrate rural areas.	Compared to their peers in urban centers, eighth-graders in rural America are 104 percent more likely to use amphetamines, including meth, 50 percent likelier to use cocaine, 83 percent likelier to use crack cocaine and 34 percent likelier to smoke marijuana.
The "redneck" myth: There are lots of pickup trucks with gun racks and people with red-colored necks.	In Idaho, a rural state, trucks account for about 85 percent of domestic auto sales. It's not much different in metropolitan Denver, where trucks account for about 80 percent of domestic auto sales.
The boredom myth: Entertainment consists of watching the cows swish away flies with their tails.	Satellite TV, radio and Internet are available everywhere and everyone has at least some access to popular culture.
The bucolic idyll myth: Seldom is heard a discouraging word and the skies are not cloudy all day.	The stresses on small town communities are incredible as some small towns become barely viable.
The political homogeneity myth: Progressive social change organizing should not waste its time there.	Withdrawing to the "blue states" would be an incredible strategic error.

To buy in to these obvious and not-so-obvious biases is to miss realities that have always been there in rural America (like Native American populations) and to miss huge trends that are altering rural America in profound and long-term ways (like Great Plains counties losing twenty percent or more of their native populations and new immigrant populations establishing a growing presence in rural communities all over the nation).

If we want to understand rural organizing clearly and understand its potential for progressive social change, then we have to look more closely. We have to pull rural communities apart and address it more specifically, not just as one big place that is simply non-urban. There are some similar trends that affect many rural areas, particularly the decline of natural resource industries, but specific regions and geographies are distinctive. Organizing in the South and organizing in the Northwest are very different endeavors. Organizing in rural New York and organizing in rural South Dakota are as different as night and day. But still, the myths live on.

Intensely rural

The parts of the country that I know best – the Northwest, West and High Plains regions – encompass every American state with a population under one million people. On this low end of the population scale, we find Idaho with around 1.2 million (slightly less than the population of New Hampshire – but spread across a huge geographic area), Montana with around 917,000, South Dakota with about 760,000, North Dakota with about 635,000 and Wyoming with about 500,000 people.

Many long-term organizers I know have been involved in fairly serious

South Dakota Population 1990 - 2000

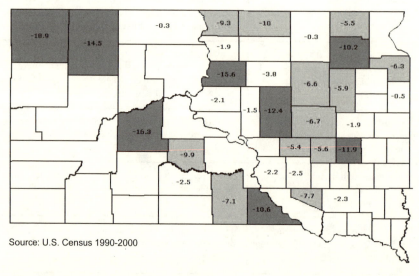

Source: U.S. Census 1990-2000

car accidents because they spend hours and hours in cars moving from one community to another. Three-hour trips are among the short drives. When I first came to Idaho, I was stunned to discover that my organization's chapter closest to Boise was two and a half hours away by car; the farthest was eight hours away. It is easier to get to Portland, Oregon, from Boise than it is to get to many parts of northern Idaho.

One five-county area of South Dakota contains 27,000 people in a geographic area the size of Connecticut. This translates to less than seven persons per square mile. There are only two libraries in those five counties. Head Start is the largest employer in one county. There are no hospitals and about eight physicians in the entire five-county area.

Two of the counties in this area lost between fourteen percent and nineteen percent of their population in a ten-year census period. That is an enormous population loss for an area with such a severely limited infrastructure. North Dakota has similar trends. This trend is so clear that when looking at national demographic maps produced by the University of North Carolina, viewers can identify the Great Plains simply by finding the counties with double-digit population losses.

Geographic areas with these population loss dynamics require a different kind of organizing than we generally think about as progressive organizers. And this kind of geography is common in much of the West, High Plains and Northwest.

In some small cities in western North Dakota, it is not possible to build a new house that will appraise for the cost required for the construction. As a result, residents cannot get a mortgage for the full amount needed to build a house in these communities. This problem is called the "appraisal gap," and it is another factor that makes finding investment in small towns extremely difficult.

Many of those same communities cannot attract a new pastor to a church that has lost its pastor. To address this situation, the United Methodist Church has assigned a number of clergy on a semi-permanent basis to serve several churches in several communities. I have talked to pastors who have three churches in their care.

One North Dakota public official used the term, "communities without a reason to live," to describe the dynamic of small town populations migrating into larger towns as jobs and public and commercial infrastructure concentrate in those larger towns. He viewed North Dakota communities with populations of fewer than one or two thousand people as barely viable over the long term.

In these rural areas, the geography defines the organizing. The geographic boundaries prescribe the form of organizing and the limited population dictates what you must do to get to scale. These dynamics also influence other factors, like a severely limited health care and other infrastructure, which can limit economic development. If a community has no health care provider and no library, it is challenging to attract a new business. The minimal tax base severely limits available public dollars, so organizing to pressure local public officials, no matter how successful, can yield few local public dollars in financial rewards.

This tends to move organizing targets up the public food chain. Thus, much rural organizing rapidly evolves to the state level where there is more to be gained.

The seeds of rural organizing success

The geography and demographic changes of rural America also contain the formula for successful organizing. Referring to the sense of connection that Wyoming residents feel with each other despite living hours and hours of driving distance apart, one state legislator stated, "Wyoming is a really just a small town with really long streets." If progressive organizing can manage to bridge geographic and constituent boundaries and create "small towns with really long streets," we can effectively achieve scale in rural organizing and enjoy organizing success.

1. **Reaching scale** – One of the concepts driving organizing is our need to "get to scale"; that is, to bring sufficient numbers of people into the public arena so we have the people power to create change. You can reach scale in rural organizing, but usually only by crossing one boundary or another.

- **No one constituency can achieve scale in rural organizing.** For instance, the Latino population in Idaho has reached almost eight percent of the total population, according to Census data, which is notorious for under-counting in communities of color. Latino people have made strides in Idaho to achieve public voice and power, but around larger issues the scale is not yet there to exert major power in the public arena.

  When major power has been exercised on Latino community issues, it has most often been in concert with other constituencies. So the lesson follows that one way to achieve scale in rural organizing is to cross constituency boundaries. One must start out with this assumption and build an organizational culture that can transcend culture and language.

- In addition, **no one community is likely to have the scale needed to leverage the resources necessary to address their local issues.** There are simply not the financial resources in most small communities and the issues are too large. Much rural organizing quickly rises to the state or federal level. This immediately creates a mutual dependency among people representing various communities. Progressive organizing needs to cross geography – travel to the next town and the next town – to organize sufficient numbers of people to achieve the scale necessary to win. However, if we do that, we can rise to state-level influence – at least in the sparsely populated states of the West.

2. **Crossing boundaries – inside and outside the organization**

- **Dynamics of distance:** Crossing the boundaries of geography, culture and language often presents a new set of issues directly into the organizing group. People from one town may feel disdain or distrust toward the people from the town down the road. That becomes an internal organizing problem.

I am asked repeatedly to attend conference calls where the majority of people are sitting around a table face to face, but I am hooked up by phone to a black box in the middle of a room. I describe the experience as akin to attending a meeting in the next room by putting my ear to the wall. No one who lives far away wants to attend every meeting in person due to the travel demand, but few feel good about being a disembodied presence in a room full of people.

We need to factor in the time, travel and communication demands on our allies and ourselves when we decide we will work with the organizations that are crossing geography to reach scale. This is a matter of basic respect.

- **Recognizing and respecting cultural differences:** People may not buy in to the organizing process unless they see leadership they trust or a sign that their culture is understood and appreciated. This can easily become an internal organizing problem.

A potential donor to an organizing drive with which I was involved in South Dakota conducted a site visit. The visitor made aggressive eye contact and directed forceful and personal questions to the Lakota women seated at the table, not understanding the cultural context in which she was operating. The meeting did not go well and the sense of resentment among the Lakota women about the perceived lack of respect the donor displayed was palpable. The donor had not taken the time to learn even the basics of the local culture.

- **Overcoming language barriers:** Finally, the responsibility to dispel language barriers cannot be ignored or allowed to fall to a few bilingual leaders or staff. People may not understand meetings or may not feel comfortable or safe when operating in English. That becomes an internal organizing problem. Accommodating the language needs of constituencies a progressive organization hopes to organize is a practical matter of organizing. Having a plan for simultaneous translation, written translation of agenda materials, training materials and bulletins communicates respect.

In the disability community there is a concept called "reasonable accommodation"; that is, to accommodate the access needs of a person with disabilities in a manner that is reasonable and achievable for both the individual and the business or public entity involved. I would alter the phrase to be "respectful accommodation."

Who gets excluded?

This starts to get at the heart of the myth about pickup trucks and rednecks. Native Americans have been in rural America since before the term was coined. But few people include Native American as part of their definition of rural.

A different trend is evolving for "Indian country." The following map details Native American land bases throughout the nation. Some of the geographically largest Native American reservations exist within the boundaries of the High Plains, the West and the Northwest.

Who is Rural America? Opportunities and Considerations for Rural Progressive Organizing

Source: 2000 U.S. Census

Native American populations on reservations and in cities are on the rise. South Dakota's Native American population increased by twenty-three percent between 1990 and 2000, moving Native Americans from 7.3 to 8.3 percent of the state's population. Most of that increase occurred on reservations – the huge land masses that form part of the fabric of rural America, but are so often forgotten in national political calculations.

The population of eight counties in western South Dakota increased by more than ten percent during the 1990s; four of these counties were located in "Indian country." A fifth, Pennington County, contains Rapid City, where an increase in the Native American population also occurred.

As this population increases and reservations' land and natural resources become more coveted by United States power brokers and as tribal gaming increases the economic power of many tribes (although not many in South Dakota), Native Americans have become more politically potent in American politics. This heightens Native Americans as potential allies of progressive rural organizing.

All progressive issues play out differently in "Indian country." This is in part due to the responsibility of the United States government to the Indian Tribes as trustees, which has been established through hundreds of years of law based on the reservation system.

Tribal sovereignty defined

Syd Beane, my co-worker and an enrolled member of the Santee Sioux Tribe at Flandreau, South Dakota, states, "If you don't understand sovereignty, you can't understand organizing in Indian country. Our task is different. We are engaged in nation-building and that is a different task than most progressive organizing understands."

And, according to the website of the Saginaw Chippewa:

> An Indian Tribe is a distinct political community. A Tribe retains its inherent powers of self-government absent action by Congress to limit those powers. A State cannot limit the powers of a Tribe.
>
> The source of Tribal powers rests in its people. Tribes have had the inherent right to govern themselves "from time immemorial" (see the Worchester v. Georgia decision of 1832). Tribal governments have the same powers as the federal and state governments to regulate their internal affairs, with few exceptions. For instance, the Tribes have the power to form a government, to decide their own membership, the right to regulate property, the right to maintain law and order, the right to regulate commerce and so on.
>
> However, over the history of the Tribes' relations with the United States, Tribes have been economically devastated. Most have not had the financial means to effectively exercise their governmental powers. For some Tribes, gaming has provided the only successful means to raise funds to be able to exercise their inherent powers of self-government.
>
> Without Tribal sovereignty and the financial means to exercise powers of self-government, Tribes would not survive as Indian Nations.

Under United States treaty law, each reservation in the United States is a sovereign nation with a direct relationship with the federal government. Despite repeated and ongoing attempts by state and local governments to undermine the role, power and influence of tribal governments, this fundamental principle has not changed. The federal government has a specific and ongoing responsibility to the indigenous people of the United States. This responsibility is a direct legacy of the United States government's military defeat and subjugation of Indian people.

Undermining tribal sovereignty endangers the very existence of Indian peoples as separate, linguistically and culturally distinct peoples. Health care, hunger, jobs, education, housing – any issue we would like to look at – is handled on reservations in a different way than most progressive organizers understand. In most cases, the question of how policy solutions would foster or undermine that critical tribal sovereignty is not asked before progressive policy is forwarded.

As Ruby Dunstan, a Native American woman from the Lytton band of the Nlaka'pamus people of British Columbia, Canada, reminds us of what tribal sovereignty means for her people:

> I think the most important thing is the preservation of our spirituality – what's left of it. Without spirituality, there isn't anything else. For me, spirituality means believing in who you are, what you are and practicing everything that you've been taught by your elders – how to fish, how to hunt, how to preserve those fish, how to pick the berries, how to use the berries and traditional foods. That's all part of spirituality, because if you don't have spirituality then you don't have those things. You are an empty shell.

Progressive organizing in the rural West cannot be separated from working with Native American people. Progressive organizers can view Native Americans as a potential constituency, but our policy solutions must be developed with tribal interests in mind. Housing, health care, telephone service and other infrastructure need to serve as supports in building the identity and nationhood of the myriad Indian peoples. Indian people cannot be viewed as "just another low-income constituency" that will be aided by the same policy solutions.

Latino people

Latino populations are also growing all over the nation. Again, myths have to be broken to understand the trends.

In the late 1990s, the ski and hotel industries in Park City, Utah, decided that recruiting Latino people would provide an answer to their chronic labor shortages. They hired recruiters and began to bring thousands of new immigrants into Park City, where very few Latino people then lived. This was done without considering housing, education, transportation and other needs of the new Park City Latinos. Sadly, the resulting backlash from the resort community residents targeted the new Latino population, not the recruiters or industry leaders.

This is not a new story and it is not limited to Utah or the ski industry. All over the nation – in Colorado ski towns, Missouri farm towns with agricultural production plants, in rural Minnesota and in the South – Latino populations are now established far beyond the boundaries of the historic "migrant stream."

South Dakota has a growing Latino migrant working population. State planners find it difficult to determine the exact number of migrant workers due to the transient nature of migrant employment, lack of documentation and the varying definitions of a migrant worker. It is likely that there are more than ten thousand migrant workers in the eastern region of South Dakota and approximately 3,500 migrant workers in the western part of the State. This total number exceeds the census data by more than thirty percent.

This population chart demonstrates that the proportional growth populations in South Dakota are among people of color. The total numbers are small by comparison, but the trends are clear.

Progressive organizations that want to build to scale in rural areas will need

South Dakota Population by Race And Persons of Hispanic Origin 1990 – 2000

	1990	1990 (%)	2000	2000 (%)	% Change
White	637,515	91.6%	669,404	88.7%	5.0%
African-American	3,258	0.5%	4,685	0.6%	43.8%
American Indian/Alaska Native	50,575	7.3%	62,283	8.3%	23.1%
Asian or Pacific Islander	3,123	0.4%	4,639	0.6%	48.5%
Other Race	1,533	0.2%	3,677	0.5%	139.9%
Two or more races	N/A	N/A	10,156	1.3%	N/A
Total	696,004	100.0%	754,844	100.0%	8.5%
Hispanic Origin, any race	5,252	0.8%	10,903	1.4%	107.6%

Source: U.S. Bureau of the Census

to figure out the respectful level at which they can operate to accommodate language differences, to accommodate cultural differences and to accommodate new leadership that may come from a different culture or even a different town that views itself as different from other places. Operating respectfully builds trust and reflects that an organization has taken the time to figure out the culture, language needs and interests of its potential new constituency.

But this effort has to go beyond the skills and sensibilities of individual organizers or leaders. Recruiting people of color or new members from different towns is simply not enough. Instead, the organization will need to retool the way it runs its meetings, be aware and thoughtful about the atmosphere of its meetings and find a way to provide clear pathways to leadership for the new constituency.

Rural areas are not what you see on television. They are distinct and dynamic places with some major new demographic trends that create opportunities for progressive organizing. Some of those opportunities have always been there and were just not understood. To take advantage of the available opportunities, however, organizing must cross boundaries of geography, culture, race and language. Doing that effectively demands the creation of multi-constituency organizations that develop internal clarity about how to respectfully accommodate differences and share leadership across those boundaries.

Gary Sandusky is a seasoned community organizer with thirty years of experience. He is a founder of a number of community organizing groups and collaborations in the West, a father, a musician/songwriter and an outdoorsman. Gary is currently the National Director of Organizing for the Center for Community Change (CCC), a role that has required the design and launch of a national program of assistance and training for organizing groups including voter work, direct technical assistance, coalition work and issue campaigns. He has played a number of roles during the last fifteen years at CCC, mostly involving work with and building organizations located in the Northwest, High Plains, and the intermountain West.

Up Close and Personal:
The Interpersonal Dynamics of Organizing in Rural America

By Gary Sandusky

How does a person with progressive values and a commitment to organizing choose to live and work in a place like Idaho? Why not stick with the "blue states"? After all, isn't Idaho where the white supremacists operate? Isn't that the heart of the "white homeland"? Isn't it where people drive around openly displaying rifles in the gun racks in the back window of their pickups?

I've dealt with these perceptions and misperceptions for almost twenty years, ever since my family and I moved to Boise, Idaho, so that I could take an organizing job with a group called Idaho Neighbors Network. It was 1987, about a year after the Aryan Nations had targeted a house bomb at human rights activist Bill Wassmuth and narrowly missed taking his life. There was a vital white supremacist movement. There was – and continues to be – aggressive political attacks on gay and lesbian people. There was – and is – a climate of religious conservatism and Democratic presidential candidates have little chance of success. I could understand the roots of my progressive friends' bafflement with what I was doing.

To really understand how I made a long-term commitment to organizing in some of the largest geographic and most thinly populated and conservative states in the country, you have to step back in time.

Who I am today as an organizer has roots that reach back to the place I grew up and in the way I grew up and to the people, religion, town and landscape that surrounded me. My worldview was sculpted by the scenes that stuck in my mind, the elements of different personalities I knew, the attitudes I encountered that formed my understanding of the world.

I've reflected on this topic a lot and talked about it so much that one friend of mine described me as "born in a tin tub, raised in an outhouse." Though my friend exaggerates, I truly did use an outhouse and bathe in a tin tub until I was ten years old. Then the county condemned our property and forced my Dad to build an indoor bathroom and put a leaching field on our land.

Here I am (about 1953), sitting with my older brother on the back step of the company house where I grew up, located in the tiny mining town of Leyden, Colorado.

And here is my dog Lady standing near the homemade teeter-totter my Dad built for us out of pipe and a two-by-six.

Oddly enough, while I was taking my bath in a tin tub, I often watched "Gunsmoke" on our black-and-white television. This odd juxtaposition of times and culture was simply the reality of my family and that place called Leyden – a tiny coal mining town of twenty-seven houses nestled in the foothills of the Colorado Rockies. My mother described its location as "ten miles from anywhere," but it was roughly halfway between Boulder and Golden, just west of Denver in a rural area soon to fall within the control of the burgeoning Denver suburbs.

At the turn of the twentieth century, the Leyden brothers built the town to house their coal miners. It was a cluster of identical company houses, all with pyramid-shaped corrugated tin roofs and the same tar-papered exteriors. Leyden provided the coal for the Denver tramway system, but by the early 1950s the automobile had begun its reign of supremacy and both the tramway and mines were shut down. But coal mining has quite literally left its traces all over the ranch land near Leyden and our yards were made of coal dust.

Leyden rose again from near extinction after World War II as veterans used their benefits to buy up these shells of houses and start over, creating a new community. This community ran its own store with one gas pump, its own water system, its own tiny lending library, its own Sunday school and its own annual fundraising auction. For most purposes, the life of the town was self-contained.

My parents used to recount how, during their first winter in our house in Leyden, the fierce winds coming off the Rocky Mountains would literally force snow and cold wind into the house through any opening it could find in the walls. My mother talked of chinking, as she called it – taking little strips of rags and pressing them with a spatula or screwdriver into gaps around the doors and windows to prevent the snow and cold air from coming in.

The children of Leyden grew up in a place where boundaries were clearly defined and understood. There were only twenty-seven houses. There was nowhere to go where someone didn't know you and you always ran the risk of having a report of your activities get back to your mom. We all rode the same yellow school bus. After an hour-long ride, it delivered us to the suburban school and clearly labeled us as the kids who came from Leyden.

Growing up in a town of twenty-seven houses was a good training ground for a future organizer, but I didn't know it at the time. Everybody knew you and your business. The good news in a small town is that there is a sense of closeness; the bad news is that everything is real close in a small community.

There were definitely some rules of hospitality at play in Leyden. Anyone could show up at almost any time and expect to be invited in for coffee, maybe a pastry and some talk. If you weren't sure you would be invited in, you could ask to borrow a cup of sugar or flour. No one said, "I need to check my calendar." You had to invite people in, ask them if they wanted some coffee and then you smiled and talked. My mother would complain loudly about the neighbor next door always showing up just as she was about to embark on a major cleaning project – but then they would sit and talk about their kids, their families and the neighbors.

The phone company blessed our town with service, but it was provided using something they called "a party line." The phone company ran two or three phone lines out to Leyden and made them serve all twenty-seven houses. Each main phone line was divided and shared among several families on the same party line and each family had its own custom ring. If the phone rang one long and two shorts, it was for my family. Four other families' phone numbers rang into our house, too, each with its custom ring. We all had to listen for our ring and then pick up the phone if it was for us.

However, that meant that four other "parties" also knew when our phone was ringing – all the phones functioned just like extensions in a single house do today. If they wanted to hear the latest news in another family, all a neighbor had to do was wait until the ringing stopped, signaling to them the phone had been answered and then carefully and quietly lift the phone and listen in. Anyone could hear our conversations if he chose.

Most Leyden families worked in union jobs, mostly at the railroad, the Coors beer plant in Golden, or in construction. Strikes were common. Unemployment was even more common and the ubiquitous sense of working class struggle was palpable.

On Sunday afternoons, people from Denver would drive out to observe the rural poverty, driving up and down the streets, looking at us and pointing at the tiny little houses and the kids with coal dust streaked on their faces. There wasn't enough water and no house had a lawn. To their eyes, we led an alien way of life.

The point of these reminiscences is that I learned a number of things out of my rural upbringing. These would include a strong value for justice and an intense sense of anger around class and economic inequities. But I also gleaned some instincts about people and community that have been combined with rural organizing experiences. The combination of the two experiences – growing up in a small town and organizing in cities – has given me some staying power amid the slower-paced atmosphere of organizing in the "red states." Some of these insights are summarized in this set of conclusions:

Interpersonal principles for rural organizing:

- Everything is close and personal. The person you target for action this morning may be eating at the next table in the restaurant where you have lunch at noon.

- Make sure you build strong, intentional relationships with the people you are working with so you can weather the storm. Those who live "ten miles from anywhere" must depend on their neighbors in times of trouble. When you organize, you can bet on trouble being part of the formula. If you have built a sense of community and mutual dependence within your organizing drive, you will have the support you need when the trouble comes.

- Broaden your tolerance for the people with whom you must work. In rural organizing, you have to work with those who live there and you don't have many chances to get things right. The people who live there are all you've got and if you alienate them, you will have blown your chance to work with them for a very long time. To avoid this, you must learn to tolerate and even accept people and behaviors in your rural constituency that you would not choose to tolerate in other settings.

- Things move more slowly. A campaign that takes one year in Chicago can take two or three in a rural area or small city. There are fewer resources, thinner public infrastructure, fewer options for people in rural communities and small cities, so change takes longer.

- Stick with tactics familiar to local people. In a rural town, just showing up to a meeting as a group may be viewed as an aggressive tactic. Actions you view as standard organizing practices may be way beyond what will be effective in a rural setting.

- Place is still important and that attachment to place connects people. Many people stay in rural communities whose economies are in decline because the place itself is so important to them. For many rural families, the connection to that place is a deep part of their identity and this shared bond can be an important basis for organizing.

- Rural people have good cause to be more cautious because everything is so personal. The people who profit from an unjust situation are likely to be sitting in church come Sunday alonside the victims of that injustice. Even in Boise – a city of over 200,000 – my house is a block and a half from the neighborhood Latter-Day Saints church. Some of my neighbors are members of the "right wing." My kid plays soccer on the same team with kids of core members of the political opposition and we stand on the sidelines together. This alters the political dialogue and dynamic.

- Retribution is real. The close nature of rural life means payback is personal too. You can win organizing battles only to discover you will pay personally in other ways.

- The history of rural organizing is as strong or stronger than urban organizing, but many organizers often overlook it or don't even know it. You can rely on that history, learn from it and build on it. Educate yourself.

- Organizing works in many settings, but it must be adapted to the culture, place and people you are working with.

Organizing in the Colonias of New Mexico – A Photo Essay

By Diana Bustamante

The Colonias Development Council (CDC) originated from the Farmworker Organizing Project in the late 1980s, under the auspices of the Catholic Diocese of Las Cruces, New Mexico. The group was formed to address living and working conditions of farmworkers in Doña Ana County in the southern part of the state. The CDC became an independent, 501(c)3 organization in 1996 and has continued to work with farmworkers. Over the last 19 years, it has expanded its work to include community and economic development, environmental justice, immigration and human rights and education in colonia communities.

Colonias are unincorporated settlements along the border between the United States and Mexico that lack access to basic infrastructure, such as safe water supplies, adequate sewage and safe and sanitary housing. Significant advances have been made in terms of infrastructure development, but many other challenges continue to plague colonia communities in southern New Mexico.

Building strong, committed grassroots organizations is the foundation of CDC's work. This foundation depends heavily on promotoras de comunidad, who are the first line of contact in the communities. Promotoras are apprentices to organizing and tend to come from the communities in which CDC works. Promotoras receive extensive training and support from CDC organizing staff and work to establish their own networks within their communities and with other grassroots groups in the region. The Congreso Regional de Colonias, for example, was formed a few years ago in order to provide solidarity support among colonia residents throughout the region. Members of organized groups have participated in regional and national gatherings, trainings and conferences, educational outreach campaigns, fundraising activities, academic presentations and rallies. There are many opportunities to celebrate accomplishments too. Above all, the solidarity expressed by the different colonia communities with each other is strong.

The following photo essay represents a glimpse of the work colonia leaders have organized. These photos also reflect the different communities, generations and diverse backgrounds of colonia residents. It has been through the collective leadership style that these groups have gained trust and credibility in their own communities.

Organizing in the Colonias of New Mexico – A Photo Essay

Leaders from Vecinos Unidos, Cruz Febres, Irma Castañeda and Eva Lee – *promotoras de comunidad* – giving a presentation on the successes of their work during a community 'Fiesta Mexicana'. September 2006.

Youth from Chaparral, with Cruz Hernandez, community organizer, enjoying dinner at the Fiesta Mexicana hosted by Vecinos Unidos in Chaparral, N.M. September 2006.

Organizing in the Colonias of New Mexico – A Photo Essay

New Mexico: Vecinos Unidos from Chaparral at the Dia de la Raza March in Sunland Park. This was the first time the Congreso Regional de Colonias presented its declaration of issues for colonia communities. October 2005.

Cruz Hernandez motivating people for the march at the Border Social Forum, Cd. Juarez, Chihuahua, Mexico. October 2006.

Organizing in the Colonias of New Mexico – A Photo Essay

"Orange Alert" Campaign includes a concerted educational outreach program, trainings, rallies and marches, a survey, letter-writing campaign and signature gathering for a petition against the landfill. March 2007.

Some of the residents from Chaparral and Sunland Park with CDC staff, after their presentation at the J. Paul Taylor Symposium on Social Justice, entitled "Environmental Justice? Unifying Research and Activism" at New Mexico State University. March 2007.

"Meet the Candidates Forum," hosted by Vecinos Unidos in Chaparral, New Mexico. Residents had an opportunity to meet more than 25 candidates and express their concerns. October 2006.

Organizing in the Colonias of New Mexico – A Photo Essay

Diana Bustamante, Doug Meiklejohn of the New Mexico Environmental Law Center, Bianca Encinias of the Southwest Network for Environmental and Economic Justice and author Derrick Jensen participate in a presentation on the New Mexico Environmental Justice Group at the J. Paul Taylor Symposium on Social Justice entitled "Environmental Justice? Unifying Research and Activism" at New Mexico State University. March 2007.

Diana Bustamante and Daniel Solis lead in a march to the U.S.-Mexico border in Sunland Park, New Mexico, Día de la Raza. October 2005.

Diana Bustamante grew up in a migrant and seasonal farmworker family in Arizona and worked her way through school, eventually earning a doctoral degree in sociology. She taught at various universities before coming to teach at New Mexico State University. In 1997 she became the executive director of the Colonias Development Council, which works in three southern counties of New Mexico. In 2004, Diana and two other CDC staff members in New Mexico – Rubén Núñez, a farmworker from Hatch and MaryAnn Benavidez, from Rincón – received the Leadership for a Changing World award from the Ford Foundation.

Rural Organizing in the Northern Great Plains and Rocky Mountain West

By Margaret MacDonald

In 1972, Anne Charter, Ellen Pfister and Vera Beth Johnson – three ranch women from the Bull Mountains of central Montana – got all dressed up and marched off to Washington, D.C., to talk to some powerful U.S. senators about unreclaimed strip mines and federal collusion with gigantic coal companies to displace family-owned ranches and farms.

Little did the women know they were launching a movement.

Years later, they looked back on the experience and laughed at how green they were. Still, they were effective and their efforts helped shape a grassroots community organizing model that lives on as a powerful seven-state citizens' movement through the Western Organization of Resource Councils (WORC) in Montana, North Dakota, Wyoming, Colorado, South Dakota, Idaho and Oregon.

It may surprise some that it was women who took on Washington interests on behalf of the traditionally male-dominated coal-mining labor force – but women have a long and influential history in Western American politics. Montana elected the first woman to Congress in 1916. In 1890, Wyoming became the first state to extend the vote to female citizens and Colorado followed suit three years later. Perhaps the tradition of politically motivated Western women began when scores of women filed as independent homesteaders in the Western territories, or wound up running prosperous ranches when they were widowed, but the women's leadership skills are a hallmark of early political organizing in the West.

Traditional Western women may eschew the rhetoric and trappings of the feminist movement, but they take pride in their strength and their ability to work hard. They are highly competitive and ambitious. Encouraging women to assume leadership roles is an important lesson for rural organizers in any region, but especially so in the Western states.

Strong rural community organizations can be the secret ingredient in a recipe for significant progressive reforms nationwide. The fact that some very sparsely populated but geographically large rural states manage to hold disproportionate sway in the U.S. Senate has meant that concerted efforts to swing a few key senators from Montana and Wyoming can undercut the national clout of the coal industry and tip the balance to effect major reforms in federal strip mining law.

Grassroots organizing among western South Dakota ranchers produced an important vote from Congresswoman Stephanie Herseth Sandlin in the spring of 2007, when she switched her stance on a bill to strengthen oil and gas well reclamation standards, bonding requirements, water protection and surface owners' negotiating rights. One hundred phone calls can swing a key congressional vote in the West, but one hundred phone calls do not materialize out of thin air. You need a local base to win at the state and national level and

a membership-based, chapter model provides that local base, along with the ability to take quick action when needed.

Rural residents' access to their Congressional delegation is nearly inconceivable to organizers in the more densely populated regions of the country. It provides an argument for multi-issue groups to forge wide alliances outside of their own more parochial interests as they build organizational maturity and sophistication. Rural and urban community organizations must look for shared interests and form alliances, because they can win significant gains on the national level when they do.

In the aftermath of the trip to Washington by the three ranch women, Montana and Wyoming ranchers of both genders organized themselves into chapters and adopted community organizing techniques to weigh in on strip mine reclamation laws at the state and federal level. Between 1970 and 1976, these grassroots organizations spurred the adoption of strong laws in their state legislatures and won significant victories at the federal level. Some of the issues unique to the semi-arid western ecosystem included:

- Protecting the alluvial valley floors from strip mining west of the 98th meridian. In the short-grass prairie ecosystem of the Powder River Basin, where much of the nation's strippable coal reserves lie, seemingly insignificant creeks and small rivers are surrounded by wide sub-irrigated plains that are essential for hay production. This irreplaceable hydrology cannot be restored once strip mined, so Congress enacted a law which prohibited access.

- Surface owner consent. When Western lands were settled under various homestead acts, most of the subsurface mineral rights were either retained by the federal government or given to the railroads as part of their 19th century land grants. In the late 1960s and early 1970s, many third-

or fourth-generation families woke up to discover that there was a strip mine planned for deeded land they had held for generations. Congress addressed this by requiring that companies must obtain surface owners' consent before they could strip mine the coal – even if the company held the rights to the coal. The split estate issue continues to threaten ranchers with the booming coal bed methane industry, which does not have to secure any kind of consent or agreement with the landowner before it is allowed to drill wells and dump brackish or highly saline groundwater on the property.

Other important wins included requiring strip miners to restore the land to the approximate original contour, which meant that they had to reshape the "overburden" that was removed during the mining process back into the landscape that it had disturbed; protection of the Custer National Forest of southeastern Montana; and requiring the use of diverse stands of drought-resistant native grasses in reclamation – not some hypothetical "higher and better use" like a paved parking lot or a golf course.

These wins reveal the import of a strong sense of place in motivating and defining rural organizing. Most rural people are strongly connected to their communities and the land and as organizers we need to understand, hear and appreciate this connection to be effective. When the land is abused and polluted, so are the people who depend on it. That special connection between people and their land sets rural organizing apart from other types. Rural organizers need not only to understand people but must constantly be factoring in land and water conditions. To work with land-based people you need to understand the land and all things that impact it. Organizers have found that staying in the homes of members when they travel helps them understand these families and their connection to the land.

Coal country ranchers soon realized they were in this struggle for the long haul. They recognized the need for strong, sustainable organizations that could take them through multiple campaigns related to mining and other industrial encroachments on their vital natural resources. They sought to identify and influence those in power and forged alliances with others facing similar challenges. The coal industry, despite stringent restrictions imposed by the Surface Mine Control and Reclamation Act, has not thrown in the towel and it is an ongoing struggle for agricultural people in the Northern Great Plains and for the mountain families of Appalachia to hold the large energy companies accountable for damaging streams, air quality and public infrastructure. In regions where citizens demand corporate responsibility in the coal industry, the presence of strong, durable, multi-issue organizations has been essential to any progress on behalf of the local residents and communities affected by coal mining.

Progressive organizing in the seemingly conservative strongholds of the Western U.S. may seem anomalous. But rural people who are threatened by massive energy companies and by grain and livestock cartels make pragmatic choices when faced with disempowerment and disenfranchisement. They get organized, learn strategy, form democratic organizations and stick to it over the long haul to make their communities more just, more sustainable and more participatory. And while the myth of rugged individualism plays well in stereotypical depictions of the old West, discerning organizers and leaders can uncover and build on the equally real history of interdependence. Rural organizers must recognize these conflicting narratives of independence and interdependence. Organizers and leaders can empower people by lifting up the rich heritage of "neighboring" (often used as a verb in rural settings), the tradition of providing help to the needy in times of crisis and the collective exercises of power and labor on the frontier that made a brittle and unforgiving climate and landscape home. This heritage runs the gamut from barn-raisings and annual cattle brandings to grand demonstrations of rural voting power, like the South Dakota Non-Partisan League's 1916 takeover of state government or the unlikely passage of a ballot initiative banning corporate farming after rural Nebraskans drummed up massive support in the early 1980s and overwhelmed the bill's unpopularity in Omaha.

WORC-affiliated farmers and ranchers are often motivated to defend future generations' right to live and work on the land, despite increased challenges since WORC's founding thirty-five years ago. A handful of gigantic food and agricultural corporations post billions of dollars in annual profits, while many farm and ranch families are losing money on every bushel of corn or wheat and every steer or lamb they ship off into the corporate food chain. For this reason, politically engaged family farmers recognize their common interests with wage earners in industrial and urban settings who are facing downsizing. The basic imperatives of human dignity and community well-being transcend the regional and urban/rural divide. A critical task in rural organizing is to identify the powerful decision-makers and to form alliances with others who have been adversely affected by their actions.

It may seem contradictory and surprising to those who struggle to make

ends meet in an urban environment, but the ever increasing stranglehold on farm inputs and markets exerted by a few giant food conglomerates has meant that many apparently land-rich agricultural producers barely eke out a living. More and more of them are leaving the rural landscapes and communities that they love in order to survive. Over the past thirty-five years, more and more family farms are sustained by at least one family member who takes a job in town (preferably one that provides health care benefits). The concentration of ownership and vertical integration in the food industry has put them in a position quite familiar to the miner who lived in the company house and bought groceries at the company store. As public transportation, health care providers and higher education institutions move further and further afield their lives are further impoverished and rural children's access to extracurricular sports and academic opportunities is severely restricted.

Native American lands and tribes are a major and growing force in public policy in the West and nationwide. Tribal leaders and members have proven to be valuable allies with their off-reservation neighbors on issues of clean air, water and groundwater protection, mine reclamation, livestock issues and mitigation of energy boom impacts. When two large coal-fired power plants were sited near the Northern Cheyenne Reservation in Montana in the mid-1970s, Northern Plains Resource Council ranchers and Northern Cheyenne tribal members joined together to fight for Class I air quality on the reservation. The Clean Air Act authorized tribes to designate the level of pollution they were willing to tolerate in their homelands and the Northern Cheyenne had adopted the cleanest possible air quality standard under federal law. In addition to organizing at the grassroots on the issues related to the power plants, the Tribe and Northern Plains combined forces to litigate successfully on key air quality issues. Their partnership included regular meetings, collaborative fund raising, joint strategy sessions and public media outreach and the formation of strong ties of trust and respect as they each fought for the lands they loved.

Over the years, some additional key lessons unique to organizing in rural western settings include:

- Leadership in rural communities is not always obvious. Some of the most respected opinion leaders may stay quiet in public settings, but they are the ones that people listen to and respect. In developing and supporting leaders, it is important for organizers to recognize and seek out those quiet but respected voices.

- Understand that families and neighbors may take radically different views on issues but still must live together and "make nice" long after the particular issue or fight goes away. They will go to the same church, their kids will play on the same teams, they will serve on the same co-op boards. Organizers need to be conscious of this reality as they work with members on strategy, set targets and develop tactics.

- Country hospitality is a hallmark and one of the greatest rewards of rural organizing. In Western states, where towns and farms are far-flung, it is quite normal to drive thirty to forty miles out of a remote town that has a population under 2,000 people to get to a member's or a leader's home. When you're organizing on that turf, be a gracious houseguest and learn to love the hospitality. Pitch in with chores (another important part of rural culture) and enjoy one of the rare places left in the United States where an oral culture still thrives.

Every organizer who works the long roads of the Great Plains and intermountain states can vouch for the strong traditions of hospitality. My personal best prize goes to June and Charlie Yarger and their family members and neighbors for service above and beyond the call of duty. During early February 1978, the McCone Agricultural Protection Association (MAPO) staged its annual banquet in Circle, followed by an auction, followed by a dance, followed by a midnight breakfast. Folks came from all over McCone and Dawson Counties and from places over 100 miles away like Billings (230 miles), Dickinson (160 miles) and Colstrip (140 miles). The Yargers invited a houseful of young community organizers to stay with them along with the banquet guest speaker, rancher Wally McRae and his wife, Ruth, from Colstrip. After midnight, we all drove the 15 miles from Circle to the homes of June and Charlie Yarger and Bob and Donna Yarger, with a fine snow whisking past our headlights. By morning, the entire eastern end of Montana had come to a halt in one of the most memorable blizzards in 50 years.

Drawing from her stores of meat in the freezer (the Yargers raised both beef and pork) and canned garden goods in the cellar and enough baking to at least raise the question whether June herself had cooked up the low pressure zone, they managed to house and feed eight guests from Sunday through Thursday. Coffee, cigarettes, whiskey and beer ran out, but even on Wednesday, June was serving up carrot cake with cream cheese frosting that she had frozen before company came. The phone lines were still alive and eggs, extra coffee, milk, bread and other sundries were

shared by nearby neighbors and delivered on snowmobiles. We played a lot of cards and found out who cheats and peeks. Good humor and friendships somehow survived the close quarters, thanks in large part to the good natured hospitality of June and Charlie and their daughters, Yvette (age 6) and Jennie (age 4).

Rural organizing is both extremely challenging and extremely rewarding. But for those who are fortunate enough to be accepted into the ranks, it is hard to top the beautiful, albeit long drives, the windshield friendships and story-telling and the generous hospitality in country where coyotes and cows can be more plentiful than people.

Margaret MacDonald *began her career as a community organizer in 1977 working in the Glendive field office of the Northern Plains Resource Council where, during the next ten years, she was a community organizer, research coordinator, staff director and lobbyist. She spent fifteen years as executive director of the Montana Association of Churches before returning to her roots as a regional organizer for the Western Organization of Resource Councils, where she continues to work with grassroots citizen organizations on issues that include sustainable biofuels, animal factories and local foods organizing. She is married to longtime community organizer John Smillie, campaign director for WORC. She graduated with a degree in Journalism from the University of Montana in 1974.*

The Country Roads that Created ACORN

By Wade Rathke

A fair characterization of ACORN – the Association of Community Organizations for Reform Now – over the bulk of its thirty-five-year history would be that it is an urban organization. Entering 2008, ACORN had 105 staffed offices serving over one thousand community organizations where more than 400,000 of its family members lived, worked and fought to make things better. Most of the organization's growth in recent years has involved an accelerated rate of expansion within the largest two hundred cities and metropolitan areas of the country and there is no reason to assume that the organizing program will veer off of this track in the near future.

Despite the unarguably urban nature of ACORN today, it was not always that way. ACORN traces its roots back to Little Rock, Arkansas, where it was founded in June 1970. Its first four years were spent organizing exclusively in that state, which decades ago could boast of Little Rock as its largest city at a strapping 150,000 people. ACORN's other offices in its early expansion in Arkansas included Fort Smith (population 50,000), Pine Bluff (42,000), Hot Springs (35,000), Jonesboro (23,000), West Memphis (22,000) and Stuttgart (15,000) – which often were cities in name only and on Saturday nights! ACORN's first expansion outside Arkansas was to Sioux Falls, South Dakota, in 1975 – hardly the usual beacon of bright city lights. From there we found ourselves not only in the Texas cities of Dallas and Forth Worth, but also in the rural communities surrounding the metroplex. It was the same story soon afterwards in Iowa, where being in Des Moines or Davenport did not stop you from hearing the heartbeat of the country – and where, in fact, many ACORN groups were organized to stop annexation by the cities!

That said, there are both lessons learned and debts to be acknowledged and paid.

Membership made the difference

At a crossroads in the early 1970s, ACORN made the decision to create a membership dues system as the foundation of our organizational sustainability. At the time, it was sort of a simple choice: starve or survive. Since then, we have made this system a cornerstone of our work, but the original choices were stark. As time went by, we quickly found that we could survive on a dues system, but to thrive we needed an expanding constituency from which to draw our membership. Such a base was only available in larger cities, rather than smaller communities, so gradually such default choices painted our corners smaller and smaller and pushed us into cities that were larger and larger. Nonetheless, we learned many lessons in the hardscrabble testing grounds of smaller and rural communities in Arkansas and many of these lessons cast shadows that influence us to this day.

Take the simple issue of membership dues and membership concentration as just one example. We believed in the early 1970s while we were developing the ACORN organizing model that we needed to hit a threshold of membership density in a community organizing drive of at least ten percent within the first ninety days of the organizing drive – in other words, ten percent of the households in a community would join the organization. We believed, just as old-time union organizers once thought, that if we could organize the initial ten percent, then we could leverage the entire community. Additionally, we believed that from that first concentration, we needed to "mop up" the organizing drive in a concerted push that would move the membership up to the twenty percent level in the first six-month time span and so forth to the point where theoretically, if not in every case, we could control the turf with a majority of the families as ACORN members. Any power we could build would be built on that foundation.

We did a number of organizing drives in the North Little Rock area to consolidate the model. North Little Rock was the smaller twin city to Little Rock, with maybe sixty thousand residents. One of the pivotal drives was in an area called Levy, which consisted mostly of single-family houses, virtually all-white and working-class at that time and a former incorporated city with houses and land spread this way and that until the city caught up to them.[1] Another drive that set the hook as deeply in the next round was in Mountain Pine, a hard-boiled, largely white, no-pretenses company town for Weyerhauser Paper that was built around a mill about a dozen miles up the road from Hot Springs, with perhaps a total population of less than three thousand folks. The organizing drive was built on the standard architecture of the organizing model at that time. In our naiveté, sometimes we can accomplish things that now seem surprising, but then seemed trivial. We pushed the drive and counted the numbers closely until we knew we literally "owned" the town organizationally, in the same way that the company owned the town commercially. We could mark the day when more than half of the town's residents and families were dues-paying, tub-thumping ACORN members. Mountain Pine ACORN[2] was able to make quite a mark and stir up a huge fuss around its issue, winning a string of victories of all make and manner.

But, we also found that even with the strength of that base and concentration we were dedicating huge resources, since achieving these benchmarks took one organizer's virtually full-time work. Even with 200 or 250 members paying twelve dollars-a-year dues (this was more than thirty years ago, remember – dues were $120 per year in 2005) and an organizer's pay at barely four thousand dollars per year, it was clear that it would not pay to continue to run an organizer out into the woods day after day, even when the numbers were good and we were winning, unless we could expand the base.

There quickly arose two parallel forces in Mountain Pine – the company and ACORN. The town, such as it was, depended on the mill and the company for the revenue to respond the constant demands of the organization. As push increasingly came to shove, the thin lines separating the town and the company began to blur and the usual struggle with the company – it threatened to close and move out, it red-baited the organization, it engaged in a constant harangue and counterattack – took their toll, requiring more organizer time and energy as the pressure increased on the leaders and members. The polarization was extreme.

We had similar situations in other small communities like Barling, a dozen miles south of Fort Smith and in Marianna in Lee County and College Station in Pulaski County, as well as some of the unincorporated areas around Little Rock. Leadership and loyalties were forged deeply and the struggles were intense. I can still remember listening to a leader standing up in a crowded PTA meeting way out past the Benton Highway in a rural Pulaski County community called Lawson. Without warning or preparation, he said that there were four things he believed in with all of his might – "God, country, family and ACORN" – and they had best heed all of them and listen carefully. We had hit the mother lode!

We just knew it could not be sustained. These days, we speak of these as resource and capacity questions. Then, all we knew is that there was more month than money. We didn't raise our first external money from foundations until 1974 and any external resources in the first years were cobbled together from churches here and there, voter registration and the odds and ends of internal fundraising. Simply put, we just could not afford to do rural organizing. It was not sustainable and we could not figure out how to produce the subsidies to make it work. We could boom out from an office in a city, like Little Rock or Des Moines or Dallas and pick up some ex-urban or rural organizing drive if we had a good reason, a good invitation, or a great issue, but as the main meat and potatoes, it was hats off to whoever could make it work – they were better men and women than we were. We had found that our model worked, but we could not make it work long enough to matter.

Front page from downwind to Harvard Square

Nonetheless, like drunks who could not stay away from the bottle, we never could turn down good invitations or great issues, even once we suspected we no longer really had good reasons to be organizing in rural areas if we were seriously trying to build a mass organization. The White Bluff Power Plant in 1974 was an example and one of the great and defining early ACORN campaigns, which made the organization's reputation in Arkansas and, increasingly, nationwide.

We had sparred with the Arkansas Power & Light Company in the early 1970s over utility rate increases that seemed to be annual affairs (AP&L was part of a multi-state energy consortium then called Middle South Utilities, which included companies in Mississippi and Louisiana and today also covers parts of eastern Texas as the conglomerate Entergy). The company then announced plans to build the "world's largest coal-burning power plant" on the White Bluff of the Arkansas River between Little Rock and Pine Bluff. The coal was going to be slurried down from the Powder River Basin in Wyoming and, until the line was built, would be run in long, hundred-car coal trains. The whole thing smelled wrong and once we started wading into the environmental impact statement, it became quickly apparent that we had a huge mess on our hands. There was no provision for coal scrubbers to reduce the pollution and once our research director[3] and I started getting on the phones and making some calls, we got a rough education about the impact of huge transmission lines, the downwind plume trajectory of coal particles and what it would do to people's health, crops, cattle and farm animals. This became total war.

It began almost totally as a ground war in the rural communities of farmers and ranchers that were in the downwind area on the eastern side of the Arkansas River. Organizers[4] pulled out of ACORN's Little Rock and North Little Rock offices and started working the projected particulate plume line, driving up the country roads, stopping in the fields and sitting around many a kitchen table talking with folks about what it might mean to them to have a gentle breeze of coal dust become part of their daily life. We spread a lot of paper out on those tables to show what had happened to ranchers in Canada and other places that had been in similar situations. ACORN groups were organized along these corridors with colorful names like the ACORN Protect the Land Association (POLA) and the ACORN Save Health and Property Association (SHAP). Not long before, we had done a huge organizing campaign in 1972 in Little Rock called "Save the City", so similar buttons and posters cropped up along the plume line that now said "Save the Land". These showed that this family and that one were members of ACORN and were ready to rock.

We were fighting on all fronts at that point. The major shareholders of Middle South Utilities at that time were some small, out-of-state outfits no one had ever heard of – Harvard, Yale, Columbia and the gang. We sent an organizer[5] up there as well to organize students, circulate petitions, do actions and generally raise hell with the Harvard Corporation about the impact of its investment. Harvard's student newspaper, the *Crimson*, ran daily stories and frequent editorials on the campaign.[6] After standing in the way of the world and our work for years, conducting a concerted cover-up of ACORN's organizing, the first front-page article on ACORN's work that ran in what was, at that time, the wildly self-important *Arkansas Gazette* newspaper, predictably told the story of how Harvard and others were in a snit over the pressure being exerted by ACORN community organizations around the White Bluff plant issue.

This was a mishmash combination that trumped expectations and built power deeply, changing radically the Arkansas understanding of ACORN, its base and its reach. We had finally made the shift towards being a force to be reckoned with.

AP&L could not recover to counterattack on so many different fronts. One of their most desperate ploys became one of our best tactical victories in the campaign. The public relations flacks for the company thought they had a chance to end-run us with our newly minted rural base in farm country, so they chartered a private plane to visit similar coal-powered generating plants to prove somehow that pollution could be seen as just more soil nutrients. We managed to get just enough advance notice of the itinerary of the visit to do some quick and dirty research into the history and problems of the plants in Kentucky where they were taking us. Early one morning, some of our rural leaders, some folks the company tried to round up, the PR team, some company officials and I squeezed into the plane with the press and off we went. At every stop we released horror stories on these plants, their environmental record and other problems. The concerns voiced by ACORN's POLA and SHAP leaders were devastating to what the company

had thought was their base, but which had somehow become our base.

ACORN's White Bluff campaign was one of the watershed events for ACORN, particularly coming in the same year that our members and allies ran for and won electoral control of the Pulaski County Quorum Court[7] (the county's legislative body), winning a majority of the more than four hundred seats[8] – and running on the front page of the *Washington Post*,[9] to the local media's great embarrassment. Furthermore, by the time the plant proposal wound its way through the Public Service Commission (fortunately, an elected body), the size of the plant had to be reduced, there had to be increased pollution protections (though we did not win scrubbers then) and the wild craziness and construction hubris of the proposed Wyoming-to-Arkansas slurry line was deemed financially impractical.[10] The company built a much smaller White Bluff power plant and it became one of the last of the huge investments in energy expansion rather than energy conservation. After all was said and done, ACORN had won something that no pundit, pol, or stud duck had thought possible. Things were changing in Arkansas.

ACORN calling

ACORN was also learning lessons about the value of urban-rural formations. They were forming the uniqueness of the institution and creating organization with a political profile and organizational base that could create power by breaking through the usual alignments and coalitions. The next time we tried to apply that lesson was in the same general area of central Arkansas near Redfield, which was the nearest community to the White Bluff plant on the western side of the Arkansas River between Pine Bluff and Little Rock. The target this time was the Redfield Telephone Company and this effort in 1976 was another part of the learning curve based in a rural laboratory on what might be possible for an organization like ACORN.

On the White Bluff campaign, when we had been moving organizers on both sides of the river, we stumbled on a common anachronism – a privately-owned telephone company with a limited service area in the era of the giant Bell and AT&T systems of the time. Southwestern Bell (now Bell South) had gradually either acquired or forced out of business most of the old independent telephone companies that had sprung up to wire and service communities around the country in the dawn of the universal telephone service drive. The places where the independents still existed were largely rural pockets of the country where the big system did not think it was profitable enough to take them over or compete. Redfield was just such a speck on the road. ACORN still had a group in the area and from time to time we were hearing complaints from the members about service, deposits, shutoffs and the like – the run-of-the-mill grievances that surround most utilities. The added spice was that this enterprise's owner and his family were legendary in the area for a level of capriciousness in the way they worked that for some passed as country eccentricity, but felt oppressive if you were on the receiving end of the problem.

The ACORN leadership and staff deliberately decided to go after the Redfield Telephone Company to see what we could learn in a "controlled" setting, a small area where we could understand and identify the variables clearly enough to learn something about this kind of match-up. The decision also arose from a frank internal frustration that after having been drawn through one utility campaign after another on rate increases, service practices and plant sitings, ACORN wanted to see if we could establish a different profile with the Arkansas Public Service Commission (PSC). We felt that they were essentially playing "high-low" on every bargain. We could never eliminate an entire rate increase; companies would offer us half or two-thirds of our request and still walk away with multiple millions of dollars and, obviously, guaranteed returns. Meanwhile, we had to explain to hard-pressed, financially distressed members that we had "won" – though they could damn well see that their electric, gas, or telephone bills – pick one, we fought them all – were going up. This did not work for a membership organization. We either had to force the PSC to deal with us differently, or we would have to find another venue for these fights in order to really win. Rather than responding to a utility petition for a change, we were going to see if we could operate on the offensive and bring forward the matter ourselves.

Enter Redfield Telephone. Here was a company we could match in full measure and try to move against with a comprehensive campaign for improvements on everything from service practices to rates. That was if – big if – we could organize a significant base of its users to drive the campaign and if they felt the need for change deeply enough and that they were ready to move through the country folkways of old habits, relatives and customs to take on the company. The company was not some faceless Wall Street or Little Rock entity, but a family enterprise run by the long-serving mayor of Redfield. This was the local power structure served raw and ready.

We started from the base of the existing group and then plotted out the entire service area, assigning organizers to each piece of the turf to see if organizing committees could be built in each part of the area to then move a majority of the customers. At the time, there was a famous landmark for regular travelers on the old Pine Bluff Highway where we would gather to meet to get on the same page – a drive-in built around a giant orange along the side of the road. For a long time I had a Polaroid picture that someone had snapped of three or four of the organizers[11] mugging for the camera before they hit the trail. We were pushing the drives in the summer to see if we could build the committees, develop the leadership structure, move the support and put on a large mass meeting before the end of the summer to finalize the campaign plan and engage with the company on the issues.

The organizers and leaders were curious whether things would be too "personal" for this campaign to work. Beth Butler warned others about the problem by telling the story of her first organizing drive in rural Pulaski County, outside of Jacksonville, when she asked one of the members to call her neighbors about an upcoming meeting. The woman looked at her in shock and said, "I don't think I should really do that. I don't know them well enough; I've only lived here thirteen years!"

Indeed. And here in Redfield, they would be cheek to jowl with their own, homegrown, local power structure over the issue of their phone service. But the issues turned out to be deep and the grievances heartfelt. As the first organizing committee meetings came in, the numbers were good: eighteen people meeting at a local church here, another dozen there – solid numbers in virtually all areas of the grid we had drawn for the drive.

The next problem was vexing: where can a mass organization meet in this hardscrabble, country county? No church was big enough. No school was willing. City Hall was out! We ended up deciding on a wing and a prayer to meet outside in a field near the fairgrounds at dusk, praying to our own separate gods against rain or the kind of unforgiving, blistering heat that the Arkansas delta can generate. I can still remember helping unload the folding chairs from pickup trucks and laying out the "meeting area," and I can remember even better watching the cars and trucks pull into the field in a steady stream to park as the sun started to drop down below the treetops along the highway on a thankfully long summer evening. The 150 or more people who stretched across that field – tramping the grass and cupping their ears to hear everything said by the organizing committee running the meeting – were ready to go. Importantly, they represented a huge percentage of the telephone company's users. When they took their petitions with them after voting on the issues, we could finally count the majority clearly and knew that we could pull it together to sign and seal the PSC complaint.

I will spare the gentle reader some of the details of the campaign, through the company owner breaking down in tears on the stand at the PSC hearings under pointed questioning by ACORN's general counsel, Steve Bachmann and the picture of the incident in the *Arkansas Democrat* later in the campaign was what a sports commentator would have called his "career moment." The company was forced to reform its service practices and to promise – and actually do – better.

At the end of the day, the company did not survive. We learned that even when we had a majority of the users and had a company cold, the nature of the

regulatory beast was such that unless we elected a different set of commissioners, we still could not win as complete a victory as we wanted. We changed tactics and started taking issues directly to the voters. The shadow of the Redfield Telephone campaign on those dirt roads among the pine trees and cotton fields lengthens right through ACORN's experiences on lifeline elections, district elections, votes to repeal sales taxes on food and medicine, on to the statewide and local minimum wage initiatives we run to this day in Florida, Arizona, Michigan, Ohio, New Orleans, Albuquerque and California.

Coffee, Max and the equation

When I first broke in as an organizer in Arkansas, I would go down to the Walgreens on Main Street early in the morning and have coffee from time to time with an elderly gentlemen named Max Allison, who was a legendary political organizer and operator in Arkansas. He had cut his teeth on the rough-and-tumble campaigns of "reform" politics in the state in post-war years. He had been the campaign director and political guru for every contested election Democratic Congressman Wilbur Mills ever had. He knew them all and knew where every body was buried. For the price of a cup of coffee, I was accepted after careful referrals and vetting into this klatch of people that would often include the man eventually elected as county judge. Various office seekers would come by – some successful and some who disappeared – the head of the local party and so forth. All of them were schooled in the Orval Faubus tradition of state politics that depended on county judges, county sheriffs and everything that went with them. They dated their time to when Orval, the six-term Democratic Arkansas governor, was a left-leaner and liberal and they were all on the other side of the 1954 Central High School racial divide. Max specialized in the old school tricks of the rural South, like running someone with a similar name to slice off votes, flooding races with sacrificial candidates, planting stories in the press (I learned the careful reading of the daily newspapers in order to watch for the "fine hand" of Max and his minions). Max and his people practiced country retail politics, which one could do in Arkansas in the early 1970s, rather than the wholesale urban politics of indeterminate numbers, voting blocs and goods and services. Votes were counted one by one. Max always spoke through indirection, being a man of the back room, the whispered aside, the meeting on the side of the road. He would raise hypothetical questions with me about whether I could follow what he would call the "equation." Essentially, this referred to the pieces that made up the political puzzle – where and in what combinations organizations, media, money and others fit. The rare accolade in these dawn tutorials was the nodding smile to one of his hangers-on that something bore watching, because "Wade understands the equation." Truthfully, I often had no idea what was even being discussed, but I hung in until I could either figure it out or grew impatient with it.

The country roads around central Arkansas and then later in other communities were often the crucibles where we learned what was really in the equation and how to operate successfully within it. The pieces were big and bulky, heavy and sharp, but you could see them clearly and you could tell when they were coming at you. It trained the organization, its organizers and its leaders, to identify all of the elements and add them in deliberately so that we could really make something happen and keep it from blowing up in our faces.

We learned we could not live on the back roads if we were going to build a mass organization of low- and moderate-income families, but we learned how we could combine the urban core with the exurban folks just past the city line. We learned that all of the work had the same elements and that people moved in good numbers and with a strong force when the issues were right, the leaders were in place and the organizers were on assignment, disciplined and moving. We learned to count the crowds and the votes wherever we found them. We learned to measure the tactics more carefully – often doing so twice to cut once – to make sure that they carefully fit the constituency and circumstances within the overall strategy, formation and campaign. We learned it was all hard work and that there were never any excuses or shortcuts. All together, thousands of miles and thousands of hours by hundreds of organizers built the ACORN that we still see growing today.

Drew and Rangeley

Recently, I read an article in the Sunday *Atlanta Journal-Constitution* that caught my eye because there was a picture of Drew, Mississippi – a small town in Sunflower County in the Mississippi Delta where my mother and her brothers were all raised and where my brother and I spent many a day lost like fish out of water, fresh from the urban wastelands of New Orleans. I read that the schools had lost another two hundred students and there were more layoffs in Drew. There was no longer a downtown to speak of. Population was still spiraling down. Cotton was no longer king. Several days later, there was an article in the *New York Times* about towns in the West and Midwest that were offering cash money and land if people would move there.

I have been back to the abandoned houses of the company camp on the western slope of Colorado where my brother was born and the area around Laramie, Wyoming, where I was born. I have walked into town council meetings there when they thought that there would be twenty thousand folks someday, thanks to oil shale and I have driven through five years later to see the boarded-up stores and houses on streets with nice curbs and gutters.

What is the answer in these communities? It saddens me that after more than forty years as an organizer, with the cuts and bruises to prove it, I honestly cannot puzzle the answer for communities like these that loom large in my heart, but increasingly light in my work. Organization always counts, but the economic and social forces seem so large and looming that folks seem to be clustered up and fighting in the rear guard, rather than advancing towards any victory at the front of the line.

I scratch my head. We were smart enough at ACORN to know what we could not learn, count our blessings, take our lessons learned and run. We never could figure out how to build something big that members could sustain unless there were enough of them to make it work. We could wed the country to the town, but we could never figure out how to make it work where the base was shrinking as fast as the organizing was growing. Hats off to those who could! We were grateful simply to have been taught so many lessons on so many country roads.

Wade Rathke is the founder and Chief Organizer of ACORN and SEIU Local 100. For over forty years, he has worked for and founded a series of organizations dedicated to winning social justice, workers' rights and a democracy where "the people shall rule." After beginning in the National Welfare Rights Organization (NWRO) in Massachusetts, Rathke started an initiative in Arkansas that would have a base in the general community, not just welfare recipients. This initiative grew into ACORN (Association of Community Organizations for Reform Now), the largest organization of lower-income and working families in the United States. Wade Rathke lives in New Orleans.

THE EVOLUTION OF A LEADER:
MacDonald Johnson

By Joe Szakos

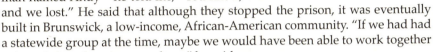

A group of people in rural Wythe County, in southwestern Virginia, stopped a private prison from coming into their community back in 1994. When I tracked down one of the key leaders of the fight – a man named Andy – he told me, "You know, we won and we lost." He said that although they stopped the prison, it was eventually built in Brunswick, a low-income, African-American community. "If we had had a statewide group at the time, maybe we would have been able to work together to keep it from locating anywhere," he said.

So I asked Andy how many other people he knew who might want to build a statewide group to work together across community boundaries. He put forty people in a room and told them about the Virginia Organizing Project's vision for long-term change and building a multi-constituency, multi-issue organization. People thought he was out of his mind, so I suggested that he start with one person at a time, slowly building relationships with a wide range of people in the community. Andy agreed, but he only went to visit in the white community, since those were the people he knew. He convinced three other people to try building an organization together. Realizing the strength of the racial divide in Wythe County, where people of color made up only about five percent of the population, I asked Andy to go talk to some of the African-American leaders in the community and see what they thought.

At that time, McDonald Johnson was an emerging leader in a local group, the African-American Concerned Citizens Network. The group had organized the African-American neighborhood and made a presentation at the town council asking for such radical things as sidewalks, curbs and paved streets. The group was being totally ignored by the town council, even though there was money in the budget for street improvements.

Andy went to visit Mac and they talked for a while about their own lives. Andy had lived in the small community for eighteen years and Mac, who was at least sixty, had lived there his whole life but they had never met before. They talked about what they wanted to see changed and they talked about why they were active in the community.

Finally Mac said, "This idea of working together sounds great. Can you get some people to show up at the town council meeting for us?" And Andy did. The town council members looked around the meeting room in disbelief. Never before had people joined together across racial lines to make a specific request of local government. In their bewilderment and fear of the unknown, the town council members said, "Sure, we'll make street and sidewalk improvements – and do whatever else we need to do."

Andy and Mac continued to build their relationship and brought other people together to do the same. They had open conversations about the racial divisions in their community, the history of the place from both the African-American and white points of view. They discussed what was and was not possible. These conversations went on for quite some time and are still going on. During this process, people also started to figure out what they wanted to see changed and what they wanted to learn in order to change things. They decided to conduct workshops on "dismantling racism," not so much to work on racial issues, but to learn how to work together.

Because there was apprehension about talking publicly about race in a place where only five percent of the people are African-American, the Virginia Organizing Project (VOP) helped organize statewide participation in the Wythe County workshops on dismantling racism. People from several communities participated in the sessions, so the focus wasn't just on one place, but rather on the broader issue of racism in many communities.

At these workshops, Mac Johnson met people from a couple of counties away who had worked together successfully on issues. They told him it could work in his community, too. Mac and a few others decided to form a core leadership group in Wythe County.

Mac also decided he wanted to learn more about the local economy. He was frustrated that his grandchildren were leaving the area to find work and he wanted to learn how to change that. He wanted to know more about how government worked, how the school board operated, how the system worked.

Some VOP leaders were meeting with the Federal Reserve Bank of Richmond on another issue at the time and Mac and Andy were invited to go to a meeting with them. Mac said, "Sure, I'll drive to Richmond and meet with them. I'll tell them what I know." Other VOP leaders helped Mac prepare for the meeting, filling him in on what he needed to know about the Federal Reserve Bank.

During the meeting, Mac and others expressed their concern about young people moving away from Wytheville to find work. A senior economic advisor with the Federal Reserve told them, "Your young people have to learn technical skills, computer skills. Get them to the community college and then tell them to move to the urban centers."

Mac objected, "I want my kids to stay near me. I want my family to be here. Why do we have to just give up on the rural economy?"

At that point, the vice president of the Federal Reserve Bank of Richmond said, "You know, you're right. With all due respect for my economist, I don't agree with him. But we don't know how to keep young people in rural communities." The Federal Reserve went on to hold a "Making Small Towns and Cities Work" conference with Mac and others in Wythe County, the first of its kind by the Fed in a rural area in Virginia.

All of a sudden Mac realized that he was involved in a process to influence how the Federal Reserve was doing its business. It gave him the confidence to go back home to continue the tedious work of a living wage campaign, going from business to business asking, "How much do you pay? How can we change this?" He had a new perspective, because he saw how wages in his community were part of a much bigger picture and that what he did could shape what that picture looked like.

As is true for all of us, Mac's life is a work in progress. People learn in different ways and come around to make commitments at different times. Some people learn a lot at "dismantling racism" workshops; others see the bigger picture and the role they have to play in it at Federal Reserve Bank meetings. Some get involved for the first time through formal training sessions; others get involved by hearing about opportunities from someone they trust over a cup of coffee.

Our organizing strategies have to include many different avenues: workshops, telephone conversations, on-site visits, reading materials, actions, conversations, videos, the whole package. And it starts with the original one-on-one conversations that ask, "Who are you? What do you want to see changed? What do you want to learn? Why are you active?"

These conversations reveal for us the direction in which people want to go – and where they will go if you ask them.

Joe Szakos has been the Executive Director of the Virginia Organizing Project since 1994. He was the Coordinator of Kentuckians For The Commonwealth from 1981 to 1993. He has also worked as a community organizer in Chicago and Hungary and has done trainings and consultations for groups throughout the United States and in Canada and Central and Eastern Europe. Joe and his wife, Kristin, are co-authors of **We Make Change: Community Organizers Talk About What They Do – And Why**, *published by Vanderbilt University Press in 2007.*

Keys to Rural Organizing – Leadership Development

By Burt Lauderdale

In 1986, the Knott County Chapter of Kentuckians For The Commonwealth (KFTC) was surging. We had members in every section of this small, underserved, very rural eastern Kentucky county. The population of Hindman, the county seat, was measured in hundreds rather than thousands. Most locals would tell you they lived along one of the creeks, like Montgomery, Lotts, Carr, Ball, or Beaver, though some would declare residence in a community or town like Mousie, Emmalena, Red Fox, Fisty, or Pippa Passes.

In spite of its small size, the county was well recognized across the state. It was home to recently deceased United States Representative Carl D. Perkins, a larger-than-life New Deal Democrat who served in Congress for thirty-six years and was praised by many and cursed by some for bringing the War on Poverty to eastern Kentucky. Local medical doctor Grady Stumbo had gained statewide notoriety with a near-miss populist campaign for governor in 1983. State Senator Benny Ray Bailey was the key strategist behind Stumbo's campaign and a major power in his own right in the Kentucky State Senate.

In addition to its political prominence, the county was known for cultural icons as diverse at the Hindman Settlement School, Alice Lloyd College, author James Still and the 1956 state basketball champions, the Carr Creek Indians.

Knott County was also known as a center of resistance to strip mining in eastern Kentucky in the 1960s when legendary local leaders like Widow Combs, Uncle Dan Gibson, Mart Shepherd and Doris Shepherd led inspired efforts to block the bulldozers from their land. They even won a local ordinance to ban strip mining in Knott County, later overturned by the state courts.

In spite of this rich history, Knott County was struggling. Roads, schools, public services and a large percentage of the people were poor. Jobs were scarce. Official unemployment figures were high, but didn't begin to tell the complete story of the long-term unemployed, the underemployed and the never employed. Only the coal industry was thriving, but thanks to mechanization and consolidation, a thriving coal industry no longer meant thriving employment for local workers.

It was in that landscape that a KFTC chapter had gotten organized in the summer of 1983, sparked primarily by interest in KFTC's efforts to stop coal companies from strip mining local landowners' property against their wishes. Coal companies had purchased the mineral rights to thousands of acres of land in central Appalachia and in Kentucky in the nineteenth and early twentieth centuries and the courts had granted the mineral owner dominance, giving them the right to strip mine without the landowner's consent. An energetic grassroots campaign that included important support in Knott County resulted in legislation in 1984 to protect the landowners. Buoyed by its victory, the Knott

County chapter surged. More people joined and began working on local issues as well as supporting statewide campaigns.

This growing local organization seemed to have something going on every week. Members attended county government meetings, researched mining permits and attended permit conferences, hosted house parties to recruit new members, organized chapter fundraisers and sponsored leadership schools where members could learn about issues and gain new organizing skills. One member and his son set up a small lab in their home, with equipment provided by KFTC and did free water testing for anyone in the county who wanted to know if their drinking water was safe.

All of this activity was possible thanks to the inspired work of a handful of local residents, none of whom had been active in the public life of their community before this experience and none of whom considered themselves leaders. Jay Conley, Orris Little, Ralph Martin, Debra Schirm, Iva and Alfred Everidge and Rose Marie Hicks were some of the members who made this chapter of over one hundred members hum. All were critical to the success of the chapter, but none more so than Rose Marie's husband, Chalmer Ray.

Chalmer Ray Hicks had been a mechanic at a garage and, later, in an underground mine, before a terrible mining accident left him permanently disabled. On his good days, he was able to drive into town or to nearby events, but he lived with constant pain and had to be careful about his every move. He got involved with KFTC when a coal company threatened to strip mine his property and he and his family were some of the first people to directly benefit from the 1984 law that blocked coal companies from using broad form deeds to destroy people's land. (Broad form deeds were the instruments used by the coal companies to purchase minerals separately from surface land. The "broad" form of the deeds had sought to give the mineral owners rights to do just about anything with their minerals.)

Though he had a number of great qualities as a person – he was humble, kind and determined – nothing about Chalmer Ray seemed particularly unique. He was just a really good person. He was an excellent mechanic and a gregarious, friendly individual who had lived in Knott County all his life. Chalmer Ray knew just about everyone in Knott County. Because he felt that KFTC had saved his land and because he was inspired by the idea of local people organizing themselves to improve their community, he was a powerfully effective voice for KFTC. He even had his own ball cap made up with "KFTC" stitched across the front in big bold letters.

In 1986, the chapter had grown beyond the rudimentary structure that was in place and the members decided to create a chapter steering committee made up of some of the most active and committed leaders from different communities and sections of the county. Chalmer Ray was one of the first ones asked to be on it and he agreed. After the Steering Committee was formed, its members began discussing how it would operate and the need arose for someone to chair the steering committee meetings. Most people thought that Chalmer Ray would make an excellent chairperson. He was active in everything the chapter was doing, was well known and was anything but egotistical or overbearing.

I went to speak with him the day before the steering committee meeting when the elections were to be held. Though I don't remember for sure, I'm willing to bet that we talked about his dog and hunting groundhogs. And we talked about the chapter and its recent activities and about the chapter steering committee. I told him that a number of people had already said that they thought he would be a great chairperson for the steering committee and asked if he would consider taking on that job.

His reaction was immediate. He looked a little horrified and agitated and spoke to me more directly than I can remember him doing before or since. "Look Burt," he said. "You know I would do anything for KFTC. I'll help put together events, I'll organize fundraisers, I'll go to house meetings and chapter meetings and get people to join. I'll get everybody to go to Fiscal Court [county government] when we need to. I'll try to get our stuff in the newspaper and I'll help set up meetings with the politicians. But please, Burt, just don't ask me to be a leader."

I have told this story to dozens of people over the past two decades for a number of reasons. I tell it because it celebrates Chalmer Ray, who passed away a few years ago and about whom I have nothing but the fondest of memories. I tell it because I think it is ironic and makes people think. But mostly, I tell it because it illustrates so much about the art and science of grassroots leadership development, what I consider to be the most important key to successful community organizing in a rural setting.

The story about Chalmer Ray illustrates the leadership potential of every person and the impressive outcomes that can be realized when you focus organizing energy on leadership development. The story presents some of the myths about leadership that so many people accept, especially people in situations like that of Chalmer Ray. Too many people believe that leadership is something other people do, that they don't have what it takes to be a leader. They believe leadership requires an advanced education or a formal title. They believe leadership is the purview of a few elite individuals. And they believe leadership is beyond their own capacity – even if the fact is that they have already carried out many of the activities, fulfilled the duties and demonstrated the respect for others that true grassroots community leadership implies.

Authentic, compassionate, skilled and visionary grassroots leaders are the key to successful community organizing that can build a politically conscious, organized base of people to make lasting progressive change. Therefore, conscious, thoughtful leadership development is the strategy that should be at the heart of community organizing if it is going to excel. We must demystify leadership and encourage – and equip – members to take on leadership roles.

With the support of a skilled trainer, the KFTC staff in 1985 developed a leadership training handbook. The handbook proved to be one of the most useful tools we have developed in our almost quarter-century as an organization. Essentially, it was a compilation of training designs for mostly basic organizing skills. Besides being instrumental in training thousands of community grassroots leaders, the handbook proved to be a useful reference, great publicity for our model of organizing and a wonderful training tool for current and future KFTC organizers. The preface to the manual reads:

> True leadership is exercised, not studied. Everyone has the potential to lead, but most people are discouraged from taking leadership roles. Their leadership potential remains undeveloped, or worse, withers away from lack of use. Our social and economic systems prevent ordinary people from recognizing and developing their talents and skills for leadership by celebrating the rich, powerful and well-educated as leaders. Too often, society ignores the contributions of homemakers, retirees, laborers and others in making their communities better places to live. To break these barriers, KFTC's leadership training program is intended to draw out an individual's potential and encourage ongoing skill development by practice and direct application in real situations.
>
> Formal leadership training sessions provide people with a safe place to try leadership roles and test their skills before applying them in the wider community. Leadership training also diminishes the fear of being left out on a limb: since the training is done in groups, people learn to contribute their talents in a cooperative rather than a competitive or individualistic leadership style.
>
> Many people have not developed the confidence to lead. No one likes to look foolish and the fear of failure often deters people from even trying. KFTC's leadership training program is designed to encourage people to recognize the abilities they already have, practice and develop their skills and accept increasing levels of responsibility as they develop the self-confidence to try new things.

Two decades later, it is hard to improve on that statement as a summary of our view of leadership and our approach to leadership development. It introduces and begins to address important questions about leadership, about who is a leader and how to help grassroots, community leaders develop.

What is leadership?

Leadership can be generally defined as playing a pivotal role in moving a group toward an established goal. Beyond that generic description, the motives, methods and models of leadership vary widely. The shelves of libraries and bookstores are crammed with books on leadership. Many are well written, some develop cult followings and a few actually include useful and intelligent insights into leadership. But too many of them celebrate and reinforce a very individualistic theory of leadership that is ideologically neutral and values a narrow definition of winning over other types of outcomes.

Our current United States President often receives praise from pundits and pollsters for being a "strong leader," never moreso than during his re-election campaign. Though their criteria for being a strong leader are often vague, in President Bush's case they usually seem to credit his unwavering support of his own decisions (no matter how flawed), his crisp and clear delegation of responsibility to his subordinates (regardless of their competence) and his personal charisma and magnetism (no matter how manufactured).

That is not the type of leadership I am talking about and not the type of leadership that we try to foster in KFTC's leadership development program.

We agree that leadership means playing a pivotal role in moving a group toward a shared goal. But we think that leadership should be collaborative, not directive. Real leadership means reflecting and communicating the vision and values of the group and aligning your self-interest with the community's self-interest. It does not mean skillfully manipulating the community to your agenda. Perhaps the most important test of leaders is how effectively and sincerely they facilitate the emergence of other leaders.

Leadership development is important because it makes all other social change strategies – organization-building, winning issues, organizing direct actions and more – possible. Genuine leadership is much more than a set of skills. Grassroots leaders work from a growing base of knowledge, a political analysis that can be described and demonstrated and a point of view rooted in shared values and a common vision. True leadership helps us stay oriented toward a long-term goal even as we strive mightily for short-term victories. It keeps the best interests of all of us in the forefront of decision-making, while encouraging emerging voices to speak to their self-interest. Great grassroots community leadership breaks the stereotypes of leaders as technically expert, elite, powerful, wealthy individuals. It gives us other models and holds out the best opportunity for preserving and evolving our democracy.

One of the best definitions of grassroots community leadership comes from Connie White, a past chairperson of our Tennessee sister organization Save Our Cumberland Mountains, who said leadership is "taking your turn." Being a grassroots community leader is an act of responsibility and of humility, done in conjunction with other people who have and will take their turn and it is the key to organizing – particularly in rural America. But it is not easy.

Why is it hard?

In my earliest years as a community organizer, I was described, affectionately I hope, by ally and mentor organizers as having a "bowling team" organizing style. They meant that my organizing was exuberant, task- and goal-oriented and in constant motion, as in, "Come on, everybody, we're going bowling! It's gonna be fun! I'll bet you'll be great. Who needs a ride? Who else should we get to play? Who wants to be captain this month? Don't forget your bowling shoes..."

My response then was that organizing isn't that complicated. It's just really, really hard. Today, although I still value and admire the occasional bowling team organizing stylist, I have revised my position. Today, I still say that organizing is plenty hard – and that most organizing is not complicated because it's so hard just doing the straightforward stuff. But the best organizing – the organizing that holds out the promise of creating a truly democratic and just society – is both hard and complicated. That type of organizing is based upon a grassroots leadership development approach and it is hard and complex because leadership development is hard and complex.

We purposefully work with the "not-usual" suspects. We believe that it is most important to organize in the most marginalized communities, meaning that our members are primarily low- and moderate-income, systematically disenfranchised people of color and most of them are women. While these folks have the same inherent leadership potential as anyone, they are also often the folks whose leadership potential has been most severely squelched, ever since childhood.

Grassroots leadership development in a rural setting is hard because there are so few models of collaborative, self-effacing, self-replicating leadership in our society in general and in small, rural communities specifically. While the population of our area is compassionate and fair-minded, most of the institutions are hierarchical and most models of leadership are directive. It is not uncommon for people to donate money, time and material goods to KFTC while refusing to be a member because they say they are not "joiners." They are distrustful of any organization because they feel disrespected by the ones with which they have come in contact. Rural communities often resemble (or are) company towns with a dominant industry and an established, recognized, powerful elite in decision-making positions. Chalmer Ray had seen leadership in the form of politicians and coal barons, but none of them were anything like him. In addition, there is usually an understood order and a "way things are done around here." Even in cases where those dynamics are not exacerbated by issues of race or gender, it takes a huge amount of courage to stand up and represent a different point of view that challenges powerful individuals and institutions and community norms. For many people, the burden is too great, especially if their efforts are discouraged by their support networks, such as their families or churches, as often happens.

Grassroots leadership development in a rural setting is hard because realizing the legitimacy of your own leadership and pursuing social change goals flies in the face of so many cultural norms that have been ingrained in our minds. From childhood, we have been told that "you can't fight City Hall" (or, in eastern Kentucky, the county courthouse) and that "you'd best not get above your raising." These lessons identify being a social change leader as not only futile, but also unseemly. The best leadership development work confronts these lessons with a whole new worldview that emphasizes values of community and fairness and teaches strategies for getting there. It is heady and complex stuff and can sometimes be overwhelming.

And finally, grassroots leadership development in a rural setting is hard because, to paraphrase the bumper sticker, "stuff happens." Even when folks are willing, their volunteer activities must compete with family and work responsibilities and the not-infrequent family emergencies or community crises.

Yet, in spite of the challenges, it is possible for lifelong residents of small, rural communities to develop the vision, self-confidence, knowledge and skills to become incredibly effective grassroots community leaders who can produce unexpected progressive change. They do it for many reasons, including because they know right from wrong and value right more than comfort. They do it because they have been pushed to and beyond their limits of tolerance of injustice. They do it because they enjoy the unanticipated rush of working with like-minded people for a just cause. Sometimes they do it because they are stubborn – a valuable trait not to be underestimated or scorned. Stubbornness in support of justice is often described in retrospect as being visionary, most likely because it is.

And, of course, it should not be overlooked that people become effective grassroots leaders because they get involved with an organization and a program that helps them develop the vision, knowledge, skills and relationships needed for success.

The art and science of grassroots leadership development

Two people play critical roles in developing a new grassroots leader – the community organizer and another veteran grassroots leader. In our model and style of organizing, these two people work closely with potential new leaders and engage, nurture and facilitate their growth.

We find – or we are found by – folks who are either interested in our work, concerned about a specific issue, or most often, are under duress caused by some circumstance, person, or institution. They might like the image of our members lobbying in the state capital, support our campaign for more funding for education, or be threatened by a mining permit in their community. If the new person seems interested in our philosophy and supportive of our platform, we will work with them to begin organizing and if they have the additional interest and inclination, begin a parallel process of leadership development. In other circumstances, a person might be an active member for a period of time before some incident or event creates a new opportunity for them to develop into a grassroots leader, or more likely, until a more experienced leader encourages them to step up and take a leadership role.

At KFTC, we have a strong grassroots leadership development program consisting of trainings and workshops. But in addition to and in conjunction with a structured program of training opportunities, there are critical steps for the organizer and veteran leader to complete with the new leader, including:

- Help people find their voice: This is essential. It begins with simply and fully listening. Later, it might include working with people to shape their story more skillfully, help them hear how they will sound to different audiences and to learn new skills of shaping their message. But initially it is most important to be a willing and engaged audience. Learning to tell your own story with power and confidence is one of the most valuable steps in developing grassroots leadership because the experience teaches the importance of helping others find their voices.

- Help people learn about larger forces: In many instances, people have little or no reliable information about the issues, institutions and individuals that may be threatening their community or causing a hardship for them or their families. Organizers and veteran leaders help people learn about the larger forces at work in their situation, about what or who is driving those forces and how it might be possible to impact them. This can be done through group workshops on topics like the changing political landscape. Or, it can be accomplished by distributing books and readings on history or world affairs. Sending new leaders to visit ally organizations provides an opportunity to learn about a bigger context. Perhaps our most effective tactic for teaching people about the larger forces at play in their communities is taking them to the state capitol to lobby legislators and participate in the sausage factory known as the Kentucky General Assembly.

- Introduce people to others like themselves: Whether people get involved in social change organizing because of a cause or a crisis, they can feel very exposed and isolated. One of the jobs of the organizer and veteran leader is to introduce new leaders to people in similar circumstances and from similar

backgrounds so that they begin to feel more confident and comfortable.

- Introduce people to others who are not like themselves: Multi-issue social change organizing depends upon people developing a larger political analysis. One of the most effective tools in doing this is to expose new leaders to people from different backgrounds, with different family situations, or a different set of concerns. Almost invariably, people who are different from each other will find unexpected common ground and enrich each other's experience and political analyses. In this way, people learn about issues of class, race, gender, sexual orientation, religion and region and open up new possibilities for social change organizing.

- Help people challenge their own assumptions and beliefs: Authentic grassroots leaders are not developed by attempts to indoctrinate them with a set of political positions or beliefs. At KFTC, we have a vision, a mission, a set of goals and a platform that all reflect a coherent set of values and principles. We invite anyone who is committed to equality, democracy and nonviolent change to become a member. We create opportunities for people to question and be challenged about their assumptions about other people and their beliefs. The process of learning, reflecting and changing is a powerful transition for a new grassroots leader and a powerful bonding experience for a team of grassroots leaders.

- Give them access to concrete skills and information: The most public part of developing new grassroots leaders is a curriculum of trainings conducted at KFTC leadership schools. We do trainings on everything from running meetings to analyzing power to recruiting members to developing strategy and winning issues. But in addition to workshops, we share written materials, do one-on-one mentoring around specific skills, action preparation, role-playing and more.

- Have fun and build camaraderie: New leaders are the most willing, most encouraged and most energized when they are leading with others. As we learn, plan and implement, we strive to make the experience fun and we seek opportunities for people to work together in ways that build a special camaraderie. Grassroots leaders appreciate and remember writing a song or performing a skit together.

- Create opportunities for practice: All of the work of developing leaders is to enable people to lead in actual practice. We have policies, structures and methods that facilitate new leaders getting to practice their new skills and fulfill their new role as a grassroots community leader by running the organization, speaking in public and creating our campaign strategies.

- Evaluate: Evaluation is obviously important to identify ways for leaders to improve their leadership skills. It is also a great opportunity for leaders to observe and evaluate constructively the performance of other leaders. Evaluation is a pointed and productive intellectual exercise where people are reflecting on what they have learned and how it applies in practice.

- Recognize people's efforts: It is difficult to overstate how important it is to provide recognition for the special efforts that grassroots leaders put forward on behalf of their communities and organizations. Because there are so few tangible rewards, public recognition and appreciation of grassroots leaders is wise and worthwhile.

The essential motivation

Although there is an art and science to developing grassroots leaders and though other leaders and community organizers can have a great influence on a new leader's development, it is up to the individual to take advantage of their opportunities and develop their leadership. Becoming a leader requires persistence, courage, intelligence, good judgment, the support of family and friends and much more. However, what inspires and distinguishes the very best grassroots leaders more than anything else is whether they are motivated primarily by self-interest or community interest.

My grandfather grew up in a tiny town in western Michigan and stayed connected, emotionally and physically, to the town all his life. Ultimately, when he was in his eighties and after he had retired for the last time, he and my grandmother moved back to the family home that had been built by my grandfather's grandfather and occupied by different family members ever since. I still remember when he described for me the period when his hometown passed from vibrant prosperity into a period of decline – a time when the town's residents separated their self-interest from the community interest. When people stopped investing their efforts in the community first, the community suffered – and the vast majority of the individuals suffered as well.

There is a valuable lesson for community organizing to be found in my grandfather's reflections and observations. Oftentimes, grassroots organizations are described as families, but the most vibrant community organizations are more like successful small towns with lots of collaboration, deep relationships, designated roles and responsibilities, shared decision-making and the occasional small and large disagreements and grievances. The healthiest such communities, geographic or otherwise, depend on leadership – formal or informal, designated or understood – that is motivated by the community's interest first, which in turn advances their self-interest.

The very best community organizing is about building power to create positive change, but it is also about building that power with integrity and in service of the shared interest of all of us. Giving of yourself for the benefit of your community is the essential motivation and the distinguishing quality of the most effective, most productive, most inspiring grassroots community leaders. And the most effective leadership development practices expect, foster, reward and reproduce this type of inspired and inspiring community leadership.

Conclusion

KFTC has survived and thrived for more than a quarter of a century due to many factors, but thanks primarily to a string of phenomenal grassroots leaders. KFTC has helped develop and has in turn been developed by, scores of individuals who placed their communities' interests first, learned, analyzed, took risks and produced results.

The album of great grassroots leaders begins with Gladys Maynard, upon whose shoulders the entire organization rests. Sidney Cornett's personal experience and leadership helped us change the constitution of the state. Mary Jane Adams steered KFTC from start-up to statewide influence. Patty Wallace is equally skilled and comfortable schmoozing legislators, schooling governors and hiding in the bushes to catch illegal dumpers of toxic waste.

Linda Brock inspired action in her community that she organized and generated fear inside coal companies whose abuse she battled. After experiencing her wrath, persistence and organizing prowess, a local coal operator told Linda's neighbor, "I wouldn't mine coal within fifty miles of that woman."

Evelyn Williams could have taught graduate courses in grit and also taught us that if one person does not have justice, none of us has justice. Sister Marie Gangwish spent her whole life lifting others into their leadership. Patty Amburgey channeled her lifelong passion for justice and fairness into her work with KFTC.

The list goes on year after year. Aloma Burke, Dallas Blue, Charlie Morgan, Janet Brown, J.D. Miller, Ruth Colvin, Sharelle Lyons-Logan, Raleigh Adams, Jane Harrod, Robert Crutcher, Henry Riekert, Opsie Collette, Randy Wilson, Bill Wooton, Elaine Stoltzfus, Herb Smith, Jennifer Weeber, Joyce Wise and so many, many more.

Daymon Morgan joined KFTC before he moved back home to Kentucky and since has taught hundreds about the impact of modern mining and the meaning of community. Teri Blanton moved out of her poisoned community and into a role of full-time grassroots leader for more than a decade. Lamar Keys demonstrated good spirit and quiet courage as KFTC chairperson.

Today, the current generation of grassroots leaders is standing on the shoulders of those who came before, learning, listening, speaking, planning, acting and giving of themselves – and KFTC is more powerful, larger and growing faster than ever before. Veteran leaders like Janet Tucker, Doug Doerrfeld and Kirk Owens are working with newer leaders like Pam Maggard, Tayna Fogle, Truman Hurt, Dana Beasley Brown, Crystal Blackburn and Ruilly Urias to organize for a better future in Kentucky and in the world.

For some reading this who know this grassroots leadership Hall of Fame, Chalmer Ray Hicks may seem like an odd choice to lift up to demonstrate the importance and effectiveness of grassroots leadership development. Chalmer Ray never became a statewide officer of KFTC. He rarely came out of Knott County. He didn't become a statewide spokesperson or testify before the state Legislature. His name wasn't well known outside of his community.

But Chalmer Ray is an example of the great grassroots leadership that has willed and allowed KFTC to succeed. Chalmer Ray found his voice, listened to others, created common ground and collective strategy, demanded accountability from public officials and followed through. Thanks to his own determination and the support of KFTC, Chalmer Ray took his turn as a community leader and his community is the better for it.

I think often of one of my favorite quotes from Dr. Martin Luther King Jr. – "The arc of history is long, but it bends toward justice" – because it justifies hope and reminds me that we are part of history and part of progress.

The thing I find dissatisfying about the quote, however, is that it makes progress sound like a natural, almost inevitable process, like photosynthesis or ocean tides. In fact, all movement toward justice has come as a result of hard work, courage and determination to fight injustice. Though formal history has failed to capture the full story, most progress has come through the actions of organized communities led by enlightened, though often unknown, grassroots leadership.

Deliberate, principled, authentic leadership development is a key to building power for justice, because these grassroots leaders are the people who go out every day and bend the arc of history just a little more toward justice. We could use more of them, bending it together.

Burt Lauderdale is the Executive Director of Kentuckians For The Commonwealth, where he has worked since 1983. KFTC is a statewide membership-based social justice organization that uses grassroots organizing and leadership development to address a wide range of social, economic, political and environmental justice issues across Kentucky. Burt lives in southeastern Kentucky with his wife Jenny, a labor and delivery nurse at their local hospital. Burt and Jenny raised their two sons, Jasper and Colin, in Laurel County and within the family of KFTC's community of grassroots leaders.

A CONVERSATION BETWEEN LEADERS:
Teri Blanton and Tayna Fogle

By Burt Lauderdale

Leadership Development: A View from the Trenches

Teri Blanton and Tayna Fogle are both active, accomplished grassroots leaders and members of Kentuckians For The Commonwealth. Blanton is a long-time KFTC member from eastern Kentucky who has served in a number of leadership roles, including statewide chairperson and is currently a leader of KFTC's Canary Project, organizing around coal and energy issues. Fogle is a newer member and leader from Lexington, Kentucky. She is a powerful spokesperson and advocate in KFTC's current campaign to win a constitutional amendment to restore voting rights to former felons. The two grassroots leaders sat down together to talk with each other about their personal stories and their ideas about grassroots leadership development.

Teri Blanton:

I was born and grew up in Dayhoit in Harlan County, Kentucky. I was the fourth generation of my family raised in that community and my children made the fifth. I left my community at age seventeen and came back at twenty-five with two kids, thinking I was bringing them to a safe place to be raised. Then in 1989 I found out that I'd actually brought my kids to a poisoned community.

A company from Houston, Texas had operated a plant near where I lived and dumped its waste in our community from 1951 to 1987. The waste got into our drinking water and in 1989 we discovered it was contaminated with about four or five different carcinogens.

My daddy was a coal miner and coal truck driver. For a while he drove one of the buses when Harlan County had a public transportation system. But for the most part of his life he was a coal truck driver, driving from the mine to the tipple.

My mother was a working mother. When the War on Poverty came to Harlan County in the 1960s, my mother got to go back to school and get her secretarial training. After that, she got a job as a clerk at the dry cleaners.

I had three brothers and two sisters, so I was one of six children. One of my brothers died as a result of injuries he received in a coal mining accident at the Darby mine. He died from lack of health care.

One sister died from cardiac arrest. I'm raising her daughter, who is sixteen now. I've had her off and on her entire life. I think I had her lobbying for trees when she was six years old. We just got back from a lobby week in Washington, D.C. and she was fantastic. She's probably one of the few sixteen-year-olds who has experience lobbying at both the state and federal levels. She is my proudest leadership development work.

Tayna Fogle:

I was born to Mary Juanita Fogle. I was the youngest girl of eight children. I grew up in Lexington, Kentucky, went to school there and played basketball there for the University of Kentucky Lady Kats.

My mom held our family together. She was a strong lady, worked about four jobs: she ironed, cooked, worked at a tobacco factory and drove the school bus. All to make sure we were OK. One vivid memory is going to clean houses with my mom, just so I could get some quality time with her.

I believe that's where my leadership qualities first came in. My mom taught me to stand up for yourself, believe in the things you're doing and go forward.

She passed last year. I was there with her. She was so proud of me and told me that. That meant a lot. Strong woman.

I also have a brother who died—he was the first of my siblings to pass and my mother mourned for him. I have two children, Michael and Ishmael and five grandchildren.

My story took an unusual turn. In around 1985, I got into some trouble and out of that came a ten-year prison sentence that I served out at the Kentucky Correctional Institute for Women.

I always knew that I had a calling, but I just didn't know what it was. When I got out of prison, my activism started growing. I went to a meeting of People Advocating Recovery and I graduated from the WRAP House (the Women's Residential Addiction Recovery house) up in northern Kentucky. From that moment on, there was a fire inside of me. And then I became a member of Kentuckians For The Commonwealth.

Teri Blanton:

I first got involved in organizing because my family and my community were threatened by this company from Texas and its pollution. But I stayed involved and started working on all this coal mining stuff because I just can't ignore the suffering of people around me.

What's most rewarding is helping people find their voice. Being part of a big community and not feeling alone – that's very rewarding. It makes a difference when you're not standing alone. Our power is in numbers. When I'm not by myself, I'm most powerful. One of the best experiences for me is educating the community about its rights and seeing it stand together.

We were helping a couple of families in Letcher County fight to protect their small community from being buried by a valley fill. They were fighting this big coal company, trying to protect the last clean stream in their area from being destroyed. There were only a couple of families living there, but we felt like it impacted all of us.

The coal man was trying to intimidate this local person because there were only a few homes that the fill would destroy. The coal guy asked how many people would even care about that community.

"Three thousand," said the landowner – meaning the whole KFTC membership.

I live three hours away from that community and it made me so proud to hear that story. That's what KFTC is all about to me.

Tayna Fogle:

Just being able to participate in this work has had a great effect on me. It means so much to have the opportunity to work in my community toward common goals and to see the confidence my neighbors have in me.

It has been empowering to have people in prominent positions in the community listen to my input. I'm the person with the actual experience and real knowledge that's been missing from the discussion.

Meeting people from other areas with shared goals – that has had a great effect on me. I get to learn about organizing, crafting policy, lobbying – what you can and cannot do. It's like being a sponge and I get to take everything I soak up to my community.

But I can't keep any of this unless I give it back to my community. It all comes back to decent human respect, human rights and civil rights. It just basically goes back to treating people decently and telling society, "Please take your foot off my throat."

God has given me a natural ability to lead that I didn't know was there for a long time. I'll work for no money for what I believe in my innermost being, because I know this is what I'm supposed to do. The way is paved by God.

Teri Blanton:

All those things that we've been through have brought us to this point. If you've lived this stuff, you speak with credibility. Because I've been through it, I can talk about it.

The Circuit Court judge in my home county restrained me from talking about my community. It was so stupid. He said I'm not supposed to mention my community and that he couldn't believe anyone would be doing this work for no pay. He said, "Why would you do this? Why would you do this?"

I told him, "Because this is my community. These are my people."

Tayna Fogle:

We will work for no money. When you get that fire inside of you, somehow, some way, you have to do it. When the money wasn't there, somehow it would show up. The way is paved.

I've been able to speak about Kentucky in Washington, D.C., New York, Virginia. I've talked about the restoration of voting rights, Kentucky's policy and laws and about Kentuckians For The Commonwealth – with no money. It's been a great journey and I look forward to doing much, much more.

Teri Blanton:

When we started doing cross-community sharing with people from one KFTC chapter going to learn about another, we discovered that once you hear about the suffering of a fellow human being, you can no longer ignore it.

Several years ago we looked at the political landscape in Kentucky and analyzed the power structures in the state. No matter what issue we were exploring, it all came back to the same few people holding political power that were keeping us from achieving what we wanted. That's how we got more involved in registering people to vote.

Tayna Fogle:

That power analysis is such a powerful tool. It's so empowering to look at what regions of the state we need to include and get involved and whom we need to target.

Teri Blanton:

With leadership development, we take it one step further. Not only do we want people to vote, but we want people to hold those elected leaders accountable once they get into office. That's where we come in, letting people know who's out there and how they voted in the Legislature or in other capacities.

It's important to give people that kind of tool so they can make informed decisions about whom to vote for. Later you can ask, "Do you really want to keep this person in office?"

Being a leader means helping others gain the knowledge to make their own decisions.

Tayna Fogle:

Yes and being a leader means helping others become leaders too. For people to become leaders, they have to understand the causes they will represent. It means not being afraid to speak out. It takes a strong will, empathy and compassion. You have to be a good listener and have something to share.

You have to engage in the moment and not be afraid to step out of the box and onto some toes of political leaders without fear of the ramifications you might suffer for speaking out.

Lessons in Rural Organizing

By Ellen Ryan

"Contacts with others alter you, even if only a little bit. We are like chemicals: processed all day long and constantly compounded with other materials."

– Etty Hillisum, *An Interrupted Life and Letters from Westerbork*

In 1978, I got my first inkling that urban organizers might be inclined to ask rural organizers to justify the need to organize in rural communities. I was working at an organizing training session for New England VISTA volunteers at the time; about two-thirds of the eighty volunteers were assigned to urban organizations and the other third to rural ones. A boisterous contingent of the urban organizers openly derided their rural counterparts for wasting time in the bucolic hinterlands of Maine, Vermont, New Hampshire and western Massachusetts. They asserted that such places had no people, no issues, no problems and therefore no need for community organizing.

The urban organizers went on to contradict themselves about the lack of people in rural New England, asserting that the people who did live there were backward defenders of the status quo and therefore not worth organizing anyway. The rural organizers were outnumbered, but gave back as good as they got, attacking urban organizers for tinkering with neighborhood issues like stop signs and litter while paper companies ran off with what was left of New England's forests and while air pollution from the industrial Midwest drifted east to poison New England soil, air, trees, water and wildlife. Everyone agreed that the factory jobs in both cities and small towns were disappearing irrevocably, first to low-wage states in the South and later to Mexico and offshore. The urban-rural debate continued throughout the New England VISTA sessions in 1978 and 1979. At the time, I chalked it up to the love of most New Englanders for a good brawl.

Born and raised in the urban East End of Bridgeport, Connecticut, I was first attracted to the world of organizing in 1973 while doing volunteer work for the United Farmworkers (UFW) as a student at Holy Cross College in Worcester, Massachusetts. The UFW – then a California-based union struggling not only for recognition of its first contracts, but for basic decency in working conditions like portable toilets and potable drinking water in the fields – struck me as neither rural nor urban, but rather just as an organization of some of the poorest-paid, most transient and abused workers in the United States. Did the big city organizers in Hartford, Providence, Portland and New Haven really begrudge these folks – not only in California, but also in the tobacco fields, cranberry bogs and orchards of New England – the resources they needed to organize? Probably not. I figured the VISTAs were mostly young (so was I) and hadn't yet seen much of the country beyond where they had grown up. Neither had I.

My job at the New England Training Center for Community Organizers in Providence, Rhode Island, gave me reason to travel from city to city, town to town and village to village throughout the six New England states. Other than noticing that Bostonians seemed to think that Boston was the center of the universe, I didn't notice much difference among urban and rural organizations. The organizing process was similar everywhere: talk to people, ask them what they want to do, get them all in the same room, make a plan together, carry it out together and evaluate all along how well things were going. The logistics varied from place to place; farmers drove to meetings in town while many urban people walked to meetings in the neighborhood. Urban organizations in southern New England had more people of color and more diverse backgrounds and languages in their memberships than the rural organizations. In terms of economic background, both the rural and urban folks were working-class and many of them were unemployed or under-employed, dislocated workers. Urban or rural, it all looked like plain old organizing to me.

My organizing work eventually took me to occasional conferences beyond New England. At these I encountered the rural-urban controversy again, but with a new twist. Organizers from Chicago, Detroit, New York City and Philadelphia assumed that every place in New England save Boston was rural and that Boston was loaded with robber-baron rich people (as though Chicago, Detroit, New York and Philadelphia didn't have their share). I once made a pitch to a New York City-based foundation for a grant to work on arson issues in several New England cities. The foundation executive found New England boring. "Everything's so little up there."

By 1980, wanderlust took me to an organizing job based in Charlotte, North Carolina, with a new organization called Grassroots Leadership, a resource center for organizing in the South. Although my residence was in North Carolina's largest city, my job kept me on the road, driving a circuit to visit mostly rural organizations in the mountains of western North Carolina, eastern Tennessee, eastern Kentucky, as well as western Tennessee, southern Virginia and sometimes West Virginia.

Once again, I saw little difference between the urban and rural groups with which I worked along the way. In the South, too, the members were mostly working-class, with many unemployed and under-employed, displaced workers. The factory jobs that had bled out of New England into the low-wage South were already slipping away to even cheaper labor markets beyond the borders of the United States. Southern Virginia had large numbers of African-Americans. Mostly white people lived in the coal-producing mountain counties. The big city of Knoxville, Tennessee had a racially mixed population, but in contrast to southern New England, there was little ethnic diversity at the time.

Still, organizing was organizing. One listened to what people had to say, got them together in the same place. People made a plan and carried it out together and evaluated how things were going.

There were differences between the South and New England. In the South, the distances between towns were greater, the roads were less congested but, especially in the mountains, more challenging to drive. People were generally more low-key and slower in their speech. Racism took on a whole new meaning beyond the rough-and-tumble, push-and-shove politics I had known in New England. African-American people lived for the most part in a parallel society apart from whites. Although the Civil Rights Act passed in 1964 and the Voting Rights Act in 1965, it was still a tricky, unpleasant, rude, or even downright dangerous experience for many African-American people to register to vote, especially outside the big cities. People my own age had gone to segregated schools; the first generation of Southerners that had attended integrated schools was just coming of age.

Wanderlust struck again around 1984 and I took an organizing job at the Family Farm Organizing Resource Center based in St. Paul, Minnesota. Again, I lived in a big city and spent most of my time driving around, this time to meetings in the mostly Lutheran or Catholic church basements of small-town and rural Minnesota, Wisconsin, North Dakota, South Dakota and Iowa. The land there, with a few notable exceptions, was totally flat. The roads were straight and wide and the distances between towns, even houses, were far greater than anything I had ever experienced. Winter weather, even for my New England blood, was numbing. Long-time residents joked that the weather kept the riff-raff out! The only time it warmed up in the winter was just before it snowed. Snow started falling well before Thanksgiving and everything that fell stayed on the ground into April.

Most of the rural farmers were white; rural Native Americans lived mostly in and around the reservations. African-Americans could be found in the cities and while many of my neighbors in St. Paul were people of color, I rarely encountered any in my work outside the urban centers. The 1980s farm crisis I walked into in the Upper Midwest reminded me of New England and the South. Thousands of farm families had lost their farms, driven out of business by low farm prices, huge debt loads and astronomical interest rates. Small businesses

that served the farm economy folded as the farmers moved out; small towns took on the same abandoned look as inner-city commercial strips in New England and Main streets in Kentucky coal towns. The people I organized with were hard working – although I learned not to call them working class. The "prairie populist" farmers and small business owners weren't working-class from their point of view, because unlike wage-laborers, they still owned the means of production – until they lost it and took jobs anywhere they could find them, at wages too low to support their families.

The farm crisis in the rural Midwest helped me clarify my understanding of organizing and ended for me the urban-rural debate that still came up from time to time at organizing conferences and with foundation program officers. Urban organizers still cornered me in the bars at conferences and asked when I was going to stop wasting my life in places like Wanda, Minnesota and Brookings, South Dakota and other places they'd never heard of.

Organizing in the United States, anywhere in the United States, is about three things in no particular order: participation in public life, bread-and-butter economics and human rights. These three things are in no particular order because organizing, to be effective, must engage in all three at the same time. I choose the phrase "participation in public life" instead of the word "democracy" for a reason. Political democracy in most of the United States has been reduced to the casting of votes, one per qualified voter, with majority rule and the protection of minorities supposedly included somewhere. While voting in elections is extremely important, voting isn't enough. Moreover, not everyone can vote: non-citizen immigrants can't participate in elections and in some states, neither can former felons who have served their sentences and reformed their lives.

Full participation in public life implies being able to identify goals, weigh courses of action, develop strategies and work through differences both within a group and across group lines. It implies a variety of knowledge and skills that organizing usually associates with a process called leadership development. It also implies the development of concrete experience over a long period of time. Participating in the process of organizing makes it possible for voters to cast ballots based on an understanding of how the system of representative democracy works in practice and the many things that are at stake in an election. The role that organizing plays in engaging people in active participation in public life nourishes and sustains democracy in ways that can't be replaced by other institutions such as education or the media alone. This is because organizing creates voluntary associations of people who work together to get things done in the public arena.

The 1980s farm crisis in the Midwest painted in stark relief on the landscape the connections between public participation, economics and human rights, as well as the devastation wrought in all three arenas when those connections are broken. My longtime organizing partner, Julie Ristau, grew up on a Minnesota hog farm and herself farmed for a number of years as an adult. She looked out on the snow-covered rural landscape one night as we drove back to the city after a meeting and mused, "The downside of the family farm economy is that it's based on the exploitation of land, women and animals." She also knew the rural life she had grown up with was had its roots long ago in the brutal clearing away of the Native American people who had lived on the land when the first European settlers arrived.

She was reflecting on the positive aspects of the life she had experienced: small commercial farms neatly tended by extended families under often brutal weather conditions and small towns and villages with locally-owned banks, retail stores, doctors' practices, insurance and newspaper offices, radio stations, theaters, bars and farmer-owned cooperatives. She remembered towns and farmsteads filled with people who knew one another and local schools, churches and civic groups that provided social engagement as well as practical community service. But the nostalgia for this way of life didn't exclude her observation that the downside was the history of exploitation. Even in the "good old days" there was much work to be done to achieve a public life that both respected and sustained all of its members.

In terms of economics, the long, relentless concentration of wealth crushed rural communities, as it has likewise crushed urban communities. While thousands of rural people lost their land, homes, farms, small businesses, cooperatives, schools and churches, a handful of multi-national grain companies – Cargill, Archer-Daniels Midland, Con-Agra – reaped record profits. As many rural banks fell under the pressure of a crumbling local economy, Chase Manhattan (now JPMorgan Chase) and others thrived. The unrelenting motto of National People's Action leader Gale Cincotta in the 1970s was, "Reinvestment, reinvestment, reinvestment." Gale said the United States needed a Marshall Plan to rebuild its crumbling cities, just as it had reinvested to rebuild war-torn Europe in the aftermath of World War II. She was right then and a decade later she was still right and her urban analysis fit the rural landscape perfectly.

In many ways, the "big guys" who caused the crisis were in the federal government – Secretary of Agriculture Earl Butz told farmers to "get big or get out,"reflecting United States trade policy plans to export more grain. Then, President Jimmy Carter started the Soviet grain embargo, severely depressing grain prices on the international market just when United States farmers had made major investments in their operations using borrowed capital at historically high interest rates. Since my experience is primarily in the upper Midwest, which had stong laws limiting corporate farming, corporations didn't buy up farmland. Usually the "big guys" who bought land at the time were simply other family farmers, often neighbors of families who lost their own farms, who were not as over-extended with debt as others who couldn't keep pace with their debts as prices for their commodities fell.

Too often, organizing efforts based in conflicting analyses of forces causing our problems, the sources of our strengths, or the most pressing issues to address, waste energy sniping at one another. Organizations based on a race analysis take issue with those based on an economic analysis. Organizations based in the values of religious faith often haven't got the time of day for the other two. Unions often bicker among themselves instead of confronting the challenges of how best to organize workers, particularly in the face of union-busting employers and weakening government regulations that protect workers in general and their rights to organize in particular.

All organizing does some good from the point of view of the people who are doing it. One sobering observation is that the Right is doing it very effectively lately. It is organizing in opposition to taxation, public schools, gay rights and affirmative action, against the decisions of the Supreme Court and advocating for the privatization of law enforcement, prison and military functions. Meanwhile, the Freedom to Farm Act passed in 1996, knocking thousands of more farmers off their land and increasing the coffers of Cargill, Con-Agra and Archer-Daniels Midland. The United States economy lost a million jobs in the last recession as the vestiges of domestic manufacturing disappeared into younger economies offshore.

Rural organizing offers insight into all of this. Many of the same people who will fight to regenerate a small-town economy might also fight to block civil unions, depending on who catches their attention first and whether they are disposed to act out of courage or out of fear. But that's also true of urban dwellers. The same folks who will fight for public transit might also fight for an end to affirmative action. Calling people to act out of vision and courage rather than fear and greed gets more and more difficult in a mass culture rooted in consumption.

The biggest challenge is to bring people together long enough to allow them to sort out what they really want to do. No matter their economic status, most people other than monks and nuns and their equivalents have little time to engage in reflection. There is a biological limit to how much the human brain can manage and we have just about reached it.

Community organizations have been at the root of economic security during most of the nineteenth and twentieth centuries. By this I mean that specific public policies that temper our economic system's tendency to extract profits at any cost have come from the hard-fought efforts of organizing: Social Security, Medicare, banking and securities regulation, progressive taxation, floor prices and quotas on farm production, clean water and air standards, home ownership programs, college loan programs, mining reclamation standards and civil rights. Organizing – both urban and rural – now needs to turn its attention to saving, restoring and expanding these public policies which prevent unrestrained economic growth from laying waste to workers, communities and the natural environment.

Over the last thirty years, the two major political parties have abandoned most of their differences concerning economic policy. Democrats court professionals into their ranks by focusing on the so-called social issues and saying little about the economy. The Republicans also focus on the social issues and say little about the economy. Both court the wealthy and corporate interests to finance their campaigns. Meanwhile, the hard-fought economic and political victories slip away and momentum to build on them is lost. Wealth becomes concentrated in fewer and fewer hands. It's up to organizing to put back on the table focus on building an economy that factors in the needs for things like meaningful work at fair wages, clean air, clean water, quality education, health care, housing and equality in human rights. The so-called wedge issues of abortion, gun control, gay rights, immigration and pornography need to be on the table, too. But the insistence by the major political parties that these issues

matter more than anything else is just not true. Resolving our cultural differences won't save our air, our water, our jobs, our health, or our basic material ability to survive long enough to work out our cultural differences. All of these require participating in public life in a careful, reasoned way.

The professional class that Democrats now court wouldn't exist if it were not for quality education, workplace protections, voting rights and so many other hard-won public policies that are now being eroded. The United States owes its prosperity not only to hard-working Americans, but to hard-working Americans who put their energy into creating public momentum for a better life for everyone. This is done through organizing. There is a lot of work to do; the solution is not to impose the concentration of wealth and power on a global scale, but to reign in runaway profits extracted at the expense of living wages, public education, health care, retirement benefits, environmental standards and human rights. We do this by taking on and negotiating with corporate power whenever possible. We also do this by exercising our public responsibilities to make government work for and maintain a decent quality of life, not only for our own citizens, but also in consideration of people whom our economy touches around the globe.

Many of these so-called wedge issues do succeed in driving wedges within and between our organizations. Racism, classism, sexism, heterosexism and ageism abound. We need to work on these moral challenges as much as we need to work on bank regulations, free trade and every other issue under the sun. It would help to focus on the basic work of organizing, which means face-to-face relationships with and among people where they live and work. It's only through the long process of participation in public life that people are invited out of our limited experiences to appreciate the experiences and points of view of others and to develop competency in the work of confrontation and negotiation.

Many times I've been surprised about my own stereotypes and assumptions.

For example, I was surprised when a white Kentucky dairy farmer back in 1987 told me she had some posters to give me to distribute on my travels. She told me she had visited her white Republican neighbors on farms to explain to them that she had found the one and only national politician who really understood the needs of family farmers and how to change things for the better. She hoped her neighbors wouldn't mind that the politician was a Democrat. They didn't. She unrolled the poster to reveal a photograph of Jesse Jackson.

Her neighbors never had reason to think about an African-American civil rights leader as their best champion. But they listened to her and they learned and many agreed that Jesse Jackson had the story right. They supported him. The point is that we need to look for bridges, not wedges. Racism wasn't the most pressing concern of these farmers – the farm economy was. And it was true that Jesse Jackson, compared to other national candidates, had the best analysis and position on their concerns. Did this mean that the white farmers suddenly dropped the baggage of white privilege? No. Did it mean that they were challenged to re-order their thinking about race? Yes. This kind of challenge, over and over again, is a product that only building face-to-face relationships can achieve. Reading books isn't enough and reading enough books to know everything one can learn from them isn't possible. Having a personal religious conversion isn't enough. No private experience is enough. Our ideas and opinions have to be refined and tested in the fire of public life.

So as much as it's comfortable to derive our positions from well-informed or ill-informed sources that agree with us, public life – and the democratic promise – demand that people both think for themselves and argue their ideas with people who don't agree with them on everything. While taking these differences into account, we identify goals and develop plans to achieve them. The organizing process produces tension and even sometimes nonviolent conflict.

I've been organizing mostly but not exclusively in rural communities for almost thirty years; I know a lot more and can do a lot more now than I could when I started and I'm still learning. I have learned that culture varies from place to place and from group to group within and across places. Cultural differences simply exist. Focusing on differences creates tension that isn't necessarily bad. However, respect for other cultures is rooted in what our different cultural experiences bring to the broader public arena, not in one-upping one another about who has suffered the most.

What rural organizing can offer to the discussion

Shortly after Ronald Reagan came to power, I attended a conference in Washington, D.C., called to figure out what to do about federal budget cuts. After listening to various advocates decry the impending loss of everything from the Aid to Families with Dependent Children program to food stamps to Section 8 housing certificates, I commented that the poor people I knew didn't want food stamps or housing vouchers – they wanted decent work at decent pay so they could afford to feed their families and pay a mortgage. My observation was about as welcome as a skunk in the kitchen. In the uncomfortable silence, I heard in my memory the voice of one of those rural VISTA volunteers spitting a retort to an urban organizer several years before: "We're working to reopen a factory because rural people still have a sense of control over their own lives."

That may be a contribution from the experiences in rural organizing that can bring us to where we need to go. Rather than focus on how to use the government to redistribute income, as many forms of urban organizing have done, rural organizations tend to focus more on how to make capitalism work on a human scale and how to use government to hold industry accountable for protecting the environment. We do this not so that suburbanites can enjoy wilderness treks, but because the land, forests, water and air are so obviously tied to our ability to sustain any living at all. Rural organizing still tends to focus on what people are capable of producing and sustaining more than on what we have a right to consume.

Rural people may speak more slowly on average than people in cities. But taking time to think before one speaks and to listen to what others have to say is a cultural practice worth spreading. Deliberate community organizing, rather than just signing people on to campaigns, also provides an opportunity to challenge cultural practices that aren't fair. Pointedly asking the men to wash the dishes after a meeting, asking a group of black farmers to present to a group of white farmers their experience in forming a cooperative marketing plan, or asking a gay soil conservation officer to explain best land reclamation practices are practical ways to put a human face and human scale on how we all have something to contribute to making life worth living.

There are as many racist institutions in the North as in the South, at least as many sexist institutions in Boston as in Prescott, Wisconsin and certainly more homophobes in New York City than the entire population of Goodhue County, Minnesota. Building public relationships wherever we find ourselves and taking action together to make life better, isn't a rural thing or an urban thing – it's something we need to do everywhere.

*Over a span of thirty years, **Ellen Ryan** has worked as a community organizer in New England, the upper Midwest and the South. Ryan first began organizing while a volunteer for the United Farmworkers Union in 1973 and has since worked at the New England Training Center for Community Organizers, Grassroots Leadership (a resource center for organizing in the South) and the Family Farm Organizing Resource Center and Regeneration Partnership in St. Paul, Minnesota. She served as lead organizer for Virginia Organizing Project for six years and now works on environmental health issues in Augusta, Maine.*

The Women's Leadership Network: A New Approach to Community Organizing in Arkansas

By Lauren Hall

The dirt road to Maria's ranch is three miles long and climbs a hillside, winding through a thick Arkansas forest. During our brief phone conversations, Maria recommended that I allot at least twenty minutes for this final leg of the trip. I am traveling to the Arco-Iris community center near Boxley – more of an historical outpost than a town – in northwestern Arkansas, to interview Maria Moroles about her work as a community organizer in her area. There are times on the road when I wonder how I will make it back out: it is rutted and steep and I know my mobile phone lost service an hour ago. Beside me in the passenger's seat is a melting bag of ice that she requested.

At the end of the road, I come out of the woods and descend into a clearing. The landscape is dotted with small shelters and structures, farm animals and luscious gardens. It feels like an oasis in the middle of Arkansas and there is gravity in the beauty of this land. Maria and her partner Miguela are hanging a Guatemalan hammock beneath the shade of an open-air pavilion that they built. They greet me, continuing with their task, after which we share a strong handshake. Somehow I realize the importance of this meeting already. More should know the scope of her work.

Throughout the afternoon, I get a tour of the grounds, as Maria points out the structures that she has built over the years, the roundhouse where ceremonial fires are offered and the sweat lodge that embodies her traditions as a medicine woman with both indigenous Aztec and Latina roots. She shows me her home, which is powered exclusively by the sun and notes that her gardens are all organic. The entire grounds are open to her community as a place to build cultural ties and enhance the community spirit. It has been a place of refuge for women, children and people of color in the Boxley area for nearly two decades. We visit the clinic, located above the barn near her home where she performs her healing work. It is serene and welcoming and exudes a warmth beyond that of traditional doctor's offices.

Our time is spent in conversation and I ask her questions about her work as a community organizer. Her non-profit organization is called Arco-Iris and its goals are preservation of the environment, environmental education and promotion of matriarchal, indigenous cultures. From the start, however, she insists that she does not define herself in the way that I expect. Her life role is that of a curandera, a traditional Indian healer and it is through this work that she comes to know the ailments of her community.

"In my tradition of healing, the ills of my community come to my door and I try to advocate for the Latino community," she says. It just so happens that social injustices – economic and environmental justice issues – often work to make her people "sick."

"I see a diverse group of people who come from many different Spanish-speaking nations: Guatemalans, Salvadorians, Colombians, etc. Because that is my first language I am able to assist them with their problems with the laws, immigration, housing, abuse, drugs, health care, the list goes on."

Access to jobs is more limited for some than others in her area. It's difficult to find housing and health care and racial profiling is a problem as the Latino population grows. Many are without utilities. She offers this picture:

> In rural Arkansas, there are so many people that live "off the grid." There are people in these mountains that do not have electricity or running water, the education opportunities are limited and sometimes nonexistent and because we are isolated and we do not have programs to address these issues. I see a lot of suffering and the government spends so much money on war and so little on the welfare of the people. We are not protecting our future generations by providing health care and education and it is mind-boggling.

Therefore, beyond her calling as a healer, wherever there is a need for a leader, an advocate, an interpreter, a sponsor, or a representative, Maria steps up to the plate. Although it is true that her cultural experience and her spiritual path frame her understanding of social justice issues, her work mirrors that of others organizing their communities for social change.

This is where our work intersects. I've driven up from the Women's Project in Little Rock, Arkansas, an organization that has been learning how to organize communities for twenty-five years. Founded by Suzanne Pharr in 1981, the goal is social change. Through their efforts to successfully work in more rural areas of the state, a union called the Women's Leadership Network (WLN) was formed in 2006; its founding ideology reminds us that every community has its leaders and that a passion and a commitment to social change does not have to be learned in school, or passed down through a formal organization. After many years of committed approaches to organizing in rural areas with the Women's Project's limited staff, the WLN brings a new approach. By connecting women across the state, the WLN, as current Women's Project director Judy Matsuoka calls it, is an incubator for social change efforts in rural areas across Arkansas.

Maria is connected to the Women's Project because she is a natural leader in her ommunity. Her words and her presence are powerful: "We need peace and respect among peoples, respect for the earth and for each other and we also want cultural preservation and empowerment of elders, women, children, folks with differing sexual identities, differing abilities, displaced indigenous peoples and low-income and rural folks. We must evaluate our privilege to bring balance to these and to the world."

The WLN provides varying degrees of support for her organization and others across the state based on need and interest. But most importantly, they offer a model of a larger social change movement that can connect the isolated struggles of rural areas across the state, so that resources, knowledge and sentiments can be shared. Part of the process of empowerment is garnering a sense of solidarity, so that victories and trials are experienced together.

It is this goal of resonance, of interconnected awareness, that brings me from my desk in Little Rock to Maria's farm. We wonder how the local injustice faced by Maria's clients mirrors that of Asian-American immigrants in the state, that of formerly incarcerated women, that of those with diverse sexual orientations and so on. How can Maria help others organizing in rural Arkansas and vice-versa? The WLN is the Women's Project's answer to these questions.

Behind the large historic home in downtown Little Rock that is occupied by the Women's Project is a carriage house. My next interview takes me here, to our own backyard where the offices of the Asian-Pacific Cultural Resource Center are located. Wilma Houston greets me at the door, a phone to her ear and papers in hand. During our conversations, Wilma answers the phone, directs calls and answers questions in languages that I don't understand. She is busy and I wait patiently. In the meantime, she tells me her story.

Wilma Houston founded the *Asian-American Reporter*, a newspaper in its seventh year that raises important issues faced by Asian-Americans in Arkansas. It was through this experience that she realized the need for a cultural center and began working to make this happen. Now the Asian-Pacific Cultural and Resource Center is available for tutoring, translation and education on immigration issues and it houses community events, forums, seminars and festivals to unite Arkansas's Asian-American community.

"I have found that organizing in rural areas is very different from working in more urban areas," Wilma says. "Those who live in cities are more exposed to opportunities, cultures, businesses, etc., outside their home and family and therefore have more of a willingness and ability to see change. They are more responsive to issues of social justice. In rural areas, people are far from development and are less likely to have access to information."

With all of the center's accomplishments under her belt, however, Wilma worries about its future because she has found it difficult to share the leadership load and she fears that she may herself be the beginning and the end of this great work.

"I am the beginning of this organization and everything that we do has happened because I started it," she says. "I realize how important sharing leadership is, so that this barrier can be overcome."

She tells me how she has learned that trust and relationships sustain movements. Specific to her organizing community is a language barrier that is important to transcend. A social change organizer must learn in this way; it is a constant feeling-out. Working alone can be like walking with your eyes closed – you must reach for ways to assemble knowledge. The lights come on when others move with you and decisions are shared products of those who have tried before. Wilma hopes to offer what she has learned with others and through the Women's WLN, she can watch as this knowledge is passed along.

The foundations of the WLN

Judy Matsuoka explains that the Women's Project has been organizing in rural areas for a number of years, but that the process became difficult without women on the ground in particular communities. She laughs, saying The WP realizes that building a movement does not mean keeping one staff member moving! The WLN is our response to the number of issues in Arkansas and the great need for organizing for social change in rural areas, because our questions have always been, "How do we do this with a limited number of staff and how do we do this all over the state and be true to the people who live in these communities?" The WLN offers a solution by building the capacity of the women who are already in rural communities.

The WLN has two major goals, Judy explains: first, to work with women in their communities to make them more effective leaders and second, to help break the barrier of isolation that rural women face and bring them together to share their skills, their resources and also their struggles. In Arkansas we have diverse populations: Asian-American, Latino, African-American, Native American. We have populations defined by sexual orientation, disability and economic status. The WLN seeks to understand how our struggles play out in our varied communities in different ways and to circumvent any conflicts that could occur between people of color by offering a forum where people can share their histories, culture and issues. According to Judy,

> Those who live in rural communities have a strong sense of place and that place includes the people that are there, the relationships between the people and a connection to that community. Therefore, they know how their issue resonates in their community. But there is a larger picture now: we can take a look at issues in terms of a larger political analysis and ask questions like, "Who benefits when low-income people of color are at each other's throats?" People tend to see their issues on a local level, they may not see the overall patterns of oppression based on race, immigration status, gender, orientation, income and access to opportunities. We want them to develop that political analysis so that they can see these issues in a larger context.

Each month, Maria and Wilma arrive at the Women's Project for the WLN meeting. They are joined by WLN director Damita Jo Marks; Beatrice Woods, a former schoolteacher organizing for education for African-American youth in the town of England; Shirley Coleman Johnson and Debra Patton from Ashdown who represent a group called Women In Action that works to raise awareness about the increase in HIV/AIDS cases in their small community. The scene is jovial as the women gather over lunch to share stories and strengthen friendships. It is a mutual learning environment, a "sisterhood partnership," and the women are comfortable with each other, which they know is a part of the mobilization strategy. After the meal, Damita reads from her notes about the progress that the group is making and the future of the WLN. Her dialogue is heartening and educational and she recaps the goals of their meeting.

"Are we utilizing each other as best we can?" she asks the women, her partners and her friends. "Are we planning and growing from our connections to each other?"

She encourages the women to use their email list to contact each other with questions and answers. Surprisingly, access to the Internet is available to all of the women in the network – a rare advantage for rural organizers. The women update their lists and Damita suggests that more communication occur among members. As I observe this, I begin to see the state of Arkansas as a web of strings threaded through the center of the state, each reaching out to the corners and across the rivers and onto places on the map where roads are not marked. Technology plays an important role in this network, but the WLN looks to the relationships to embolden the array. These mean everything.

Janet Perkins, the former director of the Women's Project, currently serves on the board of the Southern Partners Fund (SPF), a public foundation that aids rural organizing in the South – mainly non-profit organizations that focus on organizing. We meet briefly at the Women's Project one afternoon and when she arrives, her entrance is a homecoming. Barbara L'Eplattenier, a longtime volunteer for the Women's Project's library, emerges from the back of the house at the sound of Janet's commanding voice and I see that they are old friends. After the reunion, Janet shares with me some important things that she has learned in her twenty-five years of organizing about redefining the textbook image of social change workers:

> In SPF, we continually have to pay attention to what community organizing means. A lot of the time, we find that in rural communities people have been doing organizing for years, but that this work may have started out as service work and moved from meeting the community's needs to efforts at more systemic change. We know that when we are talking about community organizing we are looking at people coming together to make systemic change in the institutions that continue to be oppressive in the community. It is about creating opportunities for leadership, not just about issues touching one person, or even one organization, but in how the community can participate in a process that will really shift the power in a community. We are always

having to review this question. You have to be flexible in the way you look at it. We have had the experience of recognizing that in order to get people involved, we have to start by taking care of their basic needs and then moving to a higher level of involvement by asking others to take on some leadership and to participate in other things that will help the community to change. We see how respect and culture are a big part of it. We want to see how people are really aware of bringing folks together, for the good of all of us. So it is not always cut and dry when you try to see community organizing, it's not like, "Aha! That's it," because it is a process based on culture, on race and experience. It may always look different.

Janet broaches the issue of sustainability of a social justice movement by alluding to what some call the "crisis of victory." She is referring to the need to keep people at the table after a resolution has come about, whether good or bad. These are the trying times. She jokes, "If somebody could create a formula for keeping people involved in social change for the long haul, they'd be rich!" Accomplishing one goal is a small part of the work toward comprehensive social justice, because the progressive social change movement is about making the largest change possible. "What we do find that's worth pointing out," she adds, "is that there really is a small pocket of people in rural communities that keep going no matter what. And they are continuously working on the issues and keeping the fire lit under stuff in their communities. It is important for these people to be lifted up and for us to find out what they use to keep the work going."

There is some good work going on around the state of Arkansas. A lot of the work over the years has changed the way people look at so many issues. I think about when I first started here at the Women's Project and I recall a lot of the connections that we made with the domestic violence community, helping to get the word out about hate crimes related to women, the gay/lesbian/bisexual organizations, the women in prison initiatives. Just to look over the years to see how things have changed around all these different issues shows what organizing can do. It can help a community to change the way they see issues which is such a valuable tool for making change.

Finally, Janet closes with some words of advice for those looking to create change in their communities.

We need to evaluate: are we respecting people, being kind, benefiting lives and making people feel valued? We should never leave a community torn up or with the same problems that are already out there. We find it difficult to talk about these issues and issues of class and privilege, racism, sexism and homophobia, but we need to check ourselves. We can have all the theories, analysis, bells and whistles to look like a social justice project, but if we are not treating people like decent human beings

The Women's Leadership Network: A New Approach to Community Organizing in Arkansas

and really struggling to keep our collective humanity intact and to figure out how to love each other in a real way, what does the work mean? We have to remember that all people have value and in order for us to have thriving communities, many of these conversations may need to take place.

The picture these women offer is one that requires a larger reading of social action in rural areas and can be understood by really viewing the interconnected relationships of any community. By seeing the intrinsic leaders, connecting them to others fighting for differing incarnations of the same right and connecting to others who have been working for years and have insights to share, we have the ability to capture a long-term passion and commitment to change that reaches over people and places and surrounds diverse issues.

"Arkansas is a poor state," Judy says. "We are never going to have the monetary resources that we need to create the change that we need, but we can work to create people resources."

Lauren Hall is currently the programs and administrative coordinator at 826 Valencia, a non-profit in San Francisco's Mission District dedicated to supporting students ages six to eighteen with their creative and expository writing skills and to helping teachers with their work. Before joining the staff at 826, she earned her bachelor's degree in American Studies from Hendrix College in Arkansas. There, Lauren was an intern at the Women's Project, where she assisted Damita Jo Marks with her work in the Women's Leadership Network and had the opportunity to meet countless inspiring women dedicated to realizing social justice in their communities.

ORGANIZING LGBT FOLKS IN THE RURAL SOUTH:
Mandy Carter

By Mandy Carter and Kristin Layng Szakos

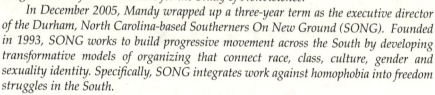

Mandy Carter is a self-described "Southern out black lesbian social justice activist." She has worked in multi-racial and multi-issue grassroots organizing for the last thirty-nine years. Her introduction to activism came in the late 1960s through the Quaker-based American Friends Service Committee, the pacifist-based War Resisters League and the former Institute for the Study of Nonviolence.

In December 2005, Mandy wrapped up a three-year term as the executive director of the Durham, North Carolina-based Southerners On New Ground (SONG). Founded in 1993, SONG works to build progressive movement across the South by developing transformative models of organizing that connect race, class, culture, gender and sexuality identity. Specifically, SONG integrates work against homophobia into freedom struggles in the South.

We asked Mandy to share some lessons she learned in getting the lesbian, gay, bisexual and transgendered (LGBT) community active in rural areas.

We have a twelve-state region that we are covering, including Arkansas, Alabama, Kentucky, North Carolina – sort of the Deep South, Louisiana, Mississippi, West Virginia, Virginia. But what we found out, especially about rural LGBT people of color, is that they did not want to be asked to come into a town like Durham or Raleigh or Chapel Hill that are more urbanized. Now, when I use the term urbanized, I'm not thinking of places like New York City or Chicago, but within the state of North Carolina, which I know best, people have this perception that if you're living in cities like Durham, Raleigh, or Charlotte, they're big cities and they feel a little bit alienated in that: "I have to come all the way from where I live out here in rural parts of eastern North Carolina to come into a big city like Durham to be part of something?"

And so when I heard that, I decided we should ask them, "What would be the best way for us to be able to get out there and talk to you? And they said, 'That's the key thing – get out here.'"

But talk about being in the closet. It's for survival if you're living in a rural area, where everyone knows you, because these are very, very small towns and farm towns. So they don't want you to come into town and have a big town meeting about being gay in rural North Carolina. Instead, they want us to come visit them personally and have one-to-one talks.

What we found out, especially with lesbians, is that they have their own networks in rural parts of North Carolina. And the way they would get their work done, if I can use that term, the way they would coordinate organizing would be through a potluck or some kind of informal social event at someone's home. They would rotate to different places and it wasn't like it was advertised anywhere, but people know who's out there. So it's the combination of being able to go to where people's homes are and finding ways in which you can ask them how they network and how you can get in on that network.

We also discovered that a lot of them didn't have computers, so this assumption that you can just automatically organize rural areas by computer is a false notion. There has to be some other kind of phone or mail contact, so you don't just rely on the Internet or email because a lot of them don't have it. It's hard, but wasn't that like organizing before we had computers?

Gay men are more likely to go to the city for socializing, where they can be anonymous, but there's still a preference that organizing be done locally, where people live.

If you're trying to organize LGBT folks in your rural community, you need someone to be a point of contact in your own backyard, understanding that you'd then get a support system going with us at SONG in Durham, so you wouldn't feel isolated. You'd have a connection with resources, information and infrastructure, so you don't have to feel like you're alone out there. That always seems to be the biggest problem: we feel so alone, so isolated, not connected. But if there are one or two people willing to serve as that initial contact person, then you have that nucleus to really start growing an infrastructure.

You also have to talk about safety measures. Ask people personally, "What concerns do you have about your own personal safety in terms of people knowing your business?" But you also have to emphasize the positives of finding ways of being connected with other folks in your community.

There's another good thing in North Carolina, particularly, in that we have an anchor organization called Equality North Carolina. They always hold at least three annual events a year, in which they try to get someone from literally every one of the 100 counties to Lobby Day (during which citizens lobby members of the state Legislature).

Some people will say, "I can't be out, but I can be labeled as a 'supporter,'" so that way the public won't know if that person is gay or straight or whatever. There are these wonderful infrastructures throughout the state, like the Pride event every September, Lobby Days in Raleigh, a faith-based network that is trying to work on LGBT issues. For a lot of people in the rural South, church is important, or faith is, so that's another avenue, another door.

There's as much of a variety among LGBT folks as anywhere. A lot of them work either farming or in the poultry industry, or in tobacco, or – before a lot of jobs went overseas – in textiles. They're just working folk.

I don't know if a single-issue LGBT organization can survive in a rural area in any kind of meaningful way. I think it's important that they get tied in with people working on other justice issues – like racism or environmental justice – a broader group that is multi-issue. People are more multi-dimensional than just being gay or lesbian; their lives are so complex and connected. I know there are attempts to try forming a single-issue gay-only group, but people say, "That's all you want to do is talk about being gay and lesbian? What about what's going to happen with my health care? Or the environmental problems facing my Latino

community?" How do you build alliances if you don't build around people's respective issues of concern?

With awards from many human rights and community organizations to acknowledge her achievements, Mandy Carter currently sits on the boards and advisory committees of the Durham-based Ladyslipper Music, the Detroit-based Triangle Foundation and the Vermont-based Kopkind Colony. She is a co-founder of the North Carolina-based Southerners On New Ground (SONG) which integrates work against homophobia into freedom struggles in the South. She is also a founding board member of the National Black Justice Coalition (NBJC) which actively pursues fairness for families and ways to counter anti-gay organzing within African-American communities. Carter has been active politically as campaign manager for efforts to unseat North Carolina Senator Jesse Helms (1990 & 1996), Florida Vote/Equal Voice voter empowerment campaign (2000) and has served as a delegate to the Democratic National Convention.

Kristin Layng Szakos *is a freelance writer/editor and the former editor of* **The Appalachian Reader**, *a quarterly journal about citizen organizing in Appalachia. She lives in Charlottesville, Virginia. Kristin and her husband, Joe are co-authors of* **We Make Change: Community Organizers Talk About What They Do — And Why**, *published by Vanderbilt University Press in 2007.*

Learning from Experience

By Steve Brooks

I was never good in school – never liked it. When I was a kid, we moved around a lot and I had to keep making new friends. At one point, we moved from a small rural town to the inner city of Cincinnati, a mostly Jewish neighborhood, which had a much better school system than any I had been in. I was put back a grade, which did not help matters.

After three years of college, I'd had all I could take and dropped out. My grades were low, but not so bad that I flunked out. I joined Volunteers In Service to America (VISTA) and began a new learning experience, later getting a degree in social psychology while I worked as a therapist.

Training

In the fall of 1968, I was trained as a VISTA organizer. They don't do it the same way anymore. It seems they don't want any college students going out into poor communities causing trouble. We were told we would be organizing poor folks to stand up for their rights.

For two weeks in Baltimore, I underwent concentrated training in how to organize in rural communities. Appalachian Volunteers, who had worked in the coalfields of Kentucky, Virginia and West Virginia, were our primary trainers. We came from all over the country but were being trained for the rural Appalachian areas of eastern Kentucky and North Carolina.

I really don't remember all that went on in those two weeks – it was mainly lots of classroom lecturing and role-playing. The main theme of instruction was that we should find out from the folks in the community what was wrong and then help them change it. In most cases we were to be placed with Community Action Agencies that already had agendas in place and we would assist them in meeting their goals. Of course, this varied a lot, with some agencies being very set in the activities they had planned for us and others that left it up to the VISTA organizers to create their own agendas.

I do remember there was a "de-selection" process. Everyone was worried about getting de-selected. They were determining which of us would not make it, who would drop out soon after being placed in the field. It was part of VISTA's mandate to maintain a low drop-out rate among the volunteers.

I think I may have come close to being de-selected. I am not a very outgoing person. I am especially poor at expressing myself in large groups of unfamiliar people. However, I had commitment and determination, which I think was also very much taken into consideration.

Because I had lived in southeastern Ohio, where there was some coal mining, I made it known my interest in being placed in eastern Kentucky. However, they wanted volunteers they determined were the best for that hotspot and so I was scheduled for travel to North Carolina.

I was very disappointed and considered dropping out. I told them so, but they would not give in – until someone who had been selected for work in Mud Creek, one of the poorest communities in eastern Kentucky, decided to quit. Without telling me right away, they decided at that point to take a chance on me. Two days before we left, they told me I was going to Kentucky.

Previous experience

I had worked in poor communities on only three previous occasions. Back in Ohio, for several years I had joined other students on weekly Friday evening visits to the Athens County Children's Home, where volunteers would play with the younger children and tutor the older ones. It was an activity organized through the Methodist Church on campus. By my sophomore year, I was the main organizer and also drove the church bus to the home and helped set up other activities for the children.

During my final year on campus, I spent spring break living with a black family in Portsmouth, Ohio. The program, run by a community action agency, was set up to place students with families in sections of town where we would work. The only thing I remember doing was participating in some kind of street cleanup during the week.

We worked with local folks, including high school-aged kids. I had a short fling with one of the girls, upsetting some of the local black boys. She later came with a group of high school kids to campus and the two of us spent more time together, getting lots of stares from many on campus. Remember, this was 1968, long before anything like that was common on Ohio campuses.

I also remember having my first taste of liquor there. One evening after the women had gone to bed, an old gentleman got out a bottle of gin and two glasses. He poured it straight and that is how we drank it. A couple shots and I was ready for bed. But we stayed up and I listened to his stories about what it used to be like and how much things had changed.

I had spent the summer before the training in Cleveland, working in what was called the "Near Westside", a white Appalachian ghetto. I worked for the Methodist Church, mostly tutoring Appalachian kids. Four or five of us college students lived in what was once the rectory, next to an old brick church that had long ago been in a very prominent middle class section of town. We also helped with a "day school" that took place in the church. We did not get too involved in social issues, though others from our group who were placed in the black community did. As far as organizing goes, we did not really do any. But it was a learning experience for me – I learned what it was like to live in the ghetto, going into homes where there was very little and conditions were very poor. I learned to communicate with folks with whom I had previously had little contact and to get to know them. I learned what some of their needs were, but at that point I did not understand how the system worked and how folks went about getting what they were being denied. It was a process in which I unconsciously learned how to talk with folks and especially how to listen and ask questions – a talent which I believe is a major part of organizing.

I have always had an easy time relating to young children. Something in me seems to attract them to me. It is usually not in words spoken, but in eye contact, just as we adults connect with each other in the same way. I have always been willing to get onto their level, both literally and figuratively. I think the same thing has to happen with adults. You have to relate at their level, whatever it is.

Eastern Kentucky

In October of 1968, four other VISTAs and I were placed in the Mud Creek Community of Floyd County in eastern Kentucky, with each of us living in the home of a local resident. I was situated at the head of Branhams Creek with a man in his sixties who ran a little country store. I stayed with him in a small four-room house next to the store, with a privy out back and running water only in the kitchen. Unlike many folks in that community, he actually had a well.

I lived there for five or six weeks, getting to know the folks that lived on this tight creek and the many hollows that ran off it. The road ended just a couple miles above us where there was a "truck mine" which employed about a half-dozen coal miners. There were several of these on the creek, with small tipples that loaded into coal trucks that then drove down to the mouth of Mud Creek and unloaded at a processing plant. There the coal was washed, sorted and then loaded into rail cars and hauled to the power plants.

After I had been in Mud Creek only a few weeks, I learned late one evening that my host sold more than groceries and dry goods from his store. We had not been in bed long when the phone rang and after a very short conversation he aroused me. He pulled a gunnysack from under his bed and told me to take it back in the woods and hide it. I did as I was told and hurried back to the house and into bed just before a state trooper and sheriff's cruiser pulled into the yard. They did a quick search of the house and store and left empty-handed. Either someone down the creek or an informer within the law enforcement system had tipped us off.

Not only was it illegal to make and sell moonshine, but no beer or alcohol of any kind was allowed to be sold in Floyd County or most of eastern Kentucky at that time. However, it could easily be obtained in many ways. Just like the selling of votes and all of the other political dealings that went on, the handling of alcohol was controlled just like in the big cities during prohibition. There was the sanctioned selling that was approved from the top (county judge and sheriff) down and sales that took place on the side in smaller amounts, such as those in which my host engaged.

Alcohol was also used as an incentive to get folks to vote the right way or to get the "boys" to carry out a task. One evening several years later when we were deeply involved in anti-strip mining activities, we got a visit from several of the "boys" from up Big Mud. They had obviously been drinking and were letting us know that we had better cease our activities or someone would get hurt. They stressed that point by waving their handguns around in the air. We told them to get the hell out of our holler and later learned that a coal mine operator had given them a case of beer in return for giving us a little scare.

We lived just down the road from a one-room schoolhouse. It was one of a handful in the county that still operated as a school, though it only went through the eighth grade. The teacher was the wife of the "power man" on the creek, the leading politician who could deliver votes to those who ran the county – which was why the school was still open. He would help folks that lived on the creek get what they needed and would then get them to vote for the "party's man" (whom he personally selected).

This was the establishment we were essentially fighting. We tried to convince the people that together they could get what they wanted and did not have to sell their vote to get it. Not a very easy task! We had to offer something in return and in this case it ended up being assistance in their legal matters and transportation to town, to doctors' offices, the store, welfare office, etc. At first we VISTA volunteers did a lot of the transporting. But later the Eastern Kentucky Welfare Rights Organization (EKWRO) got its own vehicle and hired a driver to take folks to town. We became "lay advocates," learning enough about legal rights regarding the welfare system, so we could do the initial work needed to apply for welfare benefits.

Getting to know the folks that lived in that community was the first step in organizing. The second week I was there, a group of boys took me hunting one night. There were four or five of us, one shotgun and a couple of hound dogs. We went into the woods and up the mountainside, following a steep, narrow path, as the dogs ran ahead of us.

Soon the dogs began to bark and we ran to keep up with them. I was following the others and it was all I could do to keep up with them. I feared they might want to lose me in the woods. The dogs got way ahead of us, so we slowed back down to a walk, but eventually caught up with them.

They had stopped and were barking up a tree. I was very apprehensive and somewhat frightened, as my companions had never told me what game we were hunting. I actually expected to see a bear looking down at us, but was happy to see that it was only an opossum. They were able to shake the tree and put it in a gunnysack when it fell from the branch.

Because I did not show my fear and was able to keep up with them, the boys seemed to accept me. I soon got to know them, their parents and their sisters. I began to eat dinner at various homes in the community and eventually gained their trust.

Politics

The first task we were assigned was gathering "easements" across folks' property for the placement of a water line after the 979 Community Action Agency received a grant to install a water system along the length of Mud Creek and its tributaries. We soon learned that we were there under close scrutiny, with certain restrictions placed on our activities and on us.

There were several Appalachian Volunteers working in the area, with their headquarters located in the county seat of Prestonsburg. It was not long before we met some of them and some of the local folks they were working with. They were in the process of organizing a Welfare Rights Organization specifically concerned with the lack of free school lunches at the local schools, a federal program that cost the local school system nothing. (Kids who did not bring their lunch or have money to buy it had to sit on the stage of the gymnasium, which was also the cafeteria and were thus required to watch the other children as they ate.)

The Big Sandy Community Action Program, the big daddy to the 979 Community Action Agencies, had agreed to let us come into the community, but with the understanding that we would not work with the Appalachian Volunteers. They especially did not want us to work with the Welfare Rights Organization. The five of us placed there soon agreed that we might as well go home if we did not go against their wishes.

Power in numbers

I served the two allotted years as a VISTA volunteer and then, beginning in 1970, spent two more years as one of the last Appalachian Volunteers in Kentucky. By then, the EKWRO had become a force to be reckoned with. We also began working with like-minded groups across Kentucky and eventually formed the Kentucky WRO (KWRO), which become an affiliate of the National WRO. We helped local people attend conferences in Chicago and other cities across the country. I was chosen as the director of KWRO and thus attended staff meetings in Washington, D.C. and together with other groups across the county began to apply pressure on Congress for welfare reform. (Back then, welfare reform meant making welfare available and responsive to the people who needed it – not getting rid of it altogether, like it means now!)

KWRO also gained power on the state level and was able to influence legislation that allowed low-income people access to benefits to which they were entitled. Delegates from various organizations across the state met with state welfare officials and even the governor. At one such meeting, Governor Louie Nunn invited us to return to the Capitol and have lunch with him. Two weeks later, we came with over fifty members – and when he then refused to eat and meet with us, we went to the Capitol cafeteria and ate anyway. As we moved through the line, we informed the cashier that we were the guests of the governor.

It was quite a sight to see this mix of black and white folks from both the cities and rural areas of the state, piling as much food as they could on their plates and filling all the empty tables. It was all done in a very orderly fashion, but we were not the normal folks you would expect to see in the Capitol cafeteria. When just about everyone had made it through the line, a couple guys in suits, whom we recognized as the governor's assistants, came into the cafeteria and headed to the cashier. After a short talk with her during which they pointed toward us – I was sitting with the KRWO chairwoman, a very large black woman from Louisville – they made a direct beeline to us and informed us that we would have to pay for our meals. Our chairwoman stood up and in very few words made it clear to them that no such payment would be forthcoming, as the governor had invited us as his guests and we had accepted the invitation. They high-tailed it out of there and we received neither a bill nor any further communications on the subject from the Capitol. The governor evidently chose to avoid the embarrassment of denying a meal to poor people and picked up the tab.

So what did I learn in my time in Kentucky that is useful to my organizing now? Though organizing tools have changed over the years, especially with computers and email, it still takes personal contact to make things happen. It takes time spent with folks who care and really want to do something. One must talk to them on their level and let them talk as much – or more – than you do. What really holds an organization together, I have found, is building bonds among the members. After years of working together it seems to happen, at least among a certain number of the group. This can become the core group that holds things together and makes things happen. Trying to get new folks involved is often difficult because of the tightness of this initial group. As much as one tries to attract new members, the original members can unintentionally prevent this from happening by failing to make recruits feel welcome in the group.

Conflicts inevitably will also arise among the core group and disputes are most likely to arise around money issues. When a group is first getting started and there is very little money, there is little to argue about. Strategies for actions seem to be much easier to resolve than how money is to be spent once it is acquired. I have seen more than one member leave an organization over financial matters.

In 1997, after twenty years of directing a five-county social service program, I got back into direct community organizing on both the state and local levels. I was asked to bring together a state organization of forest protection activists. This was similar to the work I did with the KWRO in the early 1970s, but also different in many ways. In both cases the local organizations already existed and I just had to bring them together and get them to cooperate on specific issues.

The work with welfare rights included folks from both rural and urban areas who were both white and black. In some cases this caused conflict, but their similar problems with the welfare system kept them together and help soothe the tensions that existed.

Working to protect Virginia's forests and communities

In my work to form the Virginia Forest Watch, the real grassroots organizing took place in local communities of southwest Virginia, where I worked to bring together folks to stop a large timber sale on national forest land. Several factors made this organizing effort a success, but it still involved lots of individual contact. Supporting our success, I believe, was the fact that many folks lived in the area affected by the proposed timbering and that excessive logging had occurred in the past. Another major factor was that the proposed sale property included two recreation areas that are very popular with the local community.

One organizing tool that we put to good use was the petition. Not long after we became aware of this proposed timber sale, we put together a petition to circulate in the communities that surround the High Knob, the mountain area where the sale was to take place. Several folks were skeptical about the effectiveness of a petition, but we went ahead with it.

We hit pay dirt with the petition one day when I was traveling up the mountain to view some of the areas to be cut. At the time I was not that familiar with the Knob and was sitting at a junction studying a map trying to figure out just where I was. A small pickup truck stopped and an older gentleman asked if I was lost. I admitted I was and he then directed me to my destination, the Bark Camp Lake.

We were about to go our separate ways when I thought to ask him if he was aware of the proposed timber sale. Noting his gun rack, I assumed he would have no problem with logging, but I was pleasantly surprised when he responded with great vigor in opposition to "more timbering" on High Knob. I asked if he would be willing to sign a petition and not only did he want to sign, he asked if I had more he could take with him. He said if I only had one that would be OK, as he could get copies made.

From that point on, the petition spread like wildfire. It turned out that he lived on the Knob not far from the Bark Camp Lake and was aware of another timber sale that was already in process. Not only was he a hunter, he was a disabled coal miner and past president of a local hunting club. A good number of the five thousand signatures that we managed to collect came to us through his efforts, as well as those of his family and friends.

At 4,223 feet, the High Knob is surrounded by many communities, some of which obtain their drinking water from streams that flow from the mountain. We started our organizing efforts by holding public meetings in four of those communities. At the meetings we presented the facts regarding the excessive timbering that had taken place in the past and shared the details of the proposed timber sale. We got the best response from the Tacoma community, where an old four-room schoolhouse was in the process of being restored and converted into a community center. It was the last of the meetings we held and there we enjoyed the largest and most vocal turnout.

It was obvious that Tacoma was the most affected by this sale, as it had been after the previous sale. The community is at the junction of United States Route 58 and one of the main access roads to High Knob, along which there are a good number of homes. It was also the community closest to the coal miner who spread the petition around. He was also responsible for getting other folks to come to this meeting.

The Clinch Coalition was formed from a follow-up meeting a few weeks later that was also held at the Tacoma center. At each meeting we had a sign-in list so were able to follow up with calls. And it took lots of calling!

For six years this group met each month. At first I made the calls, but as time went on and the secretary started to send out an email reminder each week before meetings, calls became unnecessary. But calls are important with new members and with those without computers.

After this many years, attendance has becomes a habit for many people, like going to church. But there still must be reasons to come beyond just social interaction. These folks, most of whom had not previously known each other, have become very close friends. They have traveled places together, eaten together, held press conferences together. They have not always agreed, but most of them have created strong relationships that that will keep them coming together as long as they have a purpose to do so.

Steve Brooks *is director of Virginia Forest Watch, which he helped organize in 1998. Brooks first began organizing in eastern Kentucky around welfare and environmental issues in 1968. He directed the Eastern Kentucky Welfare Rights Organization and then, after working briefly for a mental health agency, he and his wife moved to southwestern Virginia in 1975, where he worked as a tenant farmer and became active in forest issues. Steve worked for the Rural Area Development Association from 1977-1997 as director of a five-county, low-income weatherization program. He helped form the Coalition for Jobs and the Environment in 1989 and The Clinch Coalition in 1998. Steve serves on the boards of the Southern Appalachian Forest Coalition, the Upper Tennessee River Roundtable and the Southern Forest Network.*

Why Organize Rural America?

By Allen Cooper

When I started my career as an organizer, I didn't ask whether I should organize in a rural community or an urban one. I started in rural, southern West Virginia because that's where I'd grown up and I'd learned that if I wanted things to change I'd have to start the change myself. Four years later, when I moved to Austin, Texas, to organize for the Industrial Areas Foundation, I came to appreciate how unusual it is to organize in rural areas.

The currents of community organizing have followed the dominant streams of American society, to the growing cities and suburbs. Few national organizing networks in the past one hundred years have had any particular interest in rural America other than to round out a statewide strategy once the cities have been organized. In a country that is seventy-five percent urban and where the centers of commercial, industrial and financial power are located in the cities, picking urban targets is overpoweringly logical if the objective is building political power. Of course, if one's home is rural and one's objective is to have a say in public life, that logic doesn't apply. Regardless of the objective, a rural organizing project means at minimum a lot more driving for a lot less political power, on a smaller budget. Why should anyone who has a choice organize rural communities?

Thomas Jefferson and rural America

The strongest case for organizing rural America was made by Thomas Jefferson, who as author of the Declaration of Independence and the architect of the first mass-based political party is the prophet of American democracy. His preamble to the Declaration of Independence is credited with capturing the eternal truths that have motivated democratic revolutions across the globe and the steady extension of the franchise in America to women and African-Americans – the hypocrisy in his own life choices notwithstanding.

What is less recognized is that Jefferson was also the prophet of rural organizing. He believed rural America was the linchpin of American democracy and that the Declaration of Independence's democratic aspirations could be achieved only if rural America were organized. America's grand experiment in self-governance could only work, he believed, if rural communities were strong, economically independent and politically organized.

Rural America promised to solve a practical problem faced by the founders of the American Republic: how to achieve democratic self-governance on a national scale. At the time of the American Revolution, the only successful examples of democratic self-governance were on a small scale: ancient Athens about which Aristotle wrote, the early townships of New England and Native American tribal governance. Montesquieu, an influential political writer of the Enlightenment, concluded that it was not possible to achieve this kind of direct

democracy on a large scale.¹

The framers of the new nation were concerned that the governments created by the state and federal constitutions would stand as tyrants over the American people in much the same way as had King George III. Jefferson's fear was that representative bodies would be corrupted by the power concentrated in their hands and become dominated by special interests. But Jefferson and the other framers did not believe that direct democracy was a practical alternative to creating representative legislatures elected from among the people.

The framers addressed this problem in different ways. The view that carried the day and the one that rings truest to our current democratic tradition, came from James Madison. Madison accepted the power of special interests and tried to turn a weakness into a strength by arguing that in a large representative national assembly, the clash of interest groups would cancel out – or at least hobble – one another. His view was that the stronger and more varied the interest groups and the larger and more diverse the area governed by the representative body, the less likely it was that any single special interest group could run away with the power of the central government.²

In a stark contrast, Jefferson's hopeful solution to the problem was grounded in the virtues of rural America. For Jefferson, rural America was exemplified by the yeoman farmer whose virtue stemmed from his economic self-reliance. Jefferson celebrated the yeoman farmer in his *Notes on the State of Virginia*:

> Those who labour in the earth are the chosen people of God, if ever he had a chosen people, whose breasts he has made his peculiar deposit for substantial and genuine virtue. It is the focus in which he keeps alive that sacred fire, which otherwise might escape from the face of the earth. Corruption of morals in the mass of cultivators is a phenomenon of which no age nor nation has furnished an example. It is the mark set

on those, who not looking up to heaven, to their own soil and industry, as does the husbandman, of their subsistence, depend for it on the casualties and caprice of customers. Dependence begets subservience and venality, suffocates the germ of virtue and prepares fit tools for the designs of ambition.[3]

Lack of individual independence posed two risks in Jefferson's mind: He feared economic dependency might lead people to give their votes blindly to their patron, or to vote to improve their particular desperate economic condition without considering the common good. Either outcome would lead to a corrupt political process.

For Jefferson, rural America represented economic independence, whereas the manufacturing centers of early America signified the opposite. But economic independence was not enough. In a classical republican view, the economic independence of the yeoman farmer provided a basis for public virtue, but that potential virtue had to be formed through the political experience of self-governance.

Jefferson sought to maximize access to that experience by creating a ward system. Under this formula, counties would be subdivided into wards of about five square miles and comprised of one hundred families. The wards would operate as direct democracies and have responsibility for "all things relating to themselves exclusively." Each ward would operate an elementary school and administer "care of their poor, their roads, police, elections, the nomination of jurors, administration of justice in small cases, elementary exercises of militia and all those concerns which, being under their eye, they would better manage than the larger republics of the county or state."[4]

Under the ward system, people would develop their own capacities as citizens, build their commitment to democratic government, strengthen their resolve to hold their representatives at higher levels of government accountable and check their impulses to seize power. "When there shall not be a man in the State who will not be a member of some one of its councils great or small, he will let the heart be torn out of his body sooner than his power be wrested from him by a Caesar or a Bonaparte."[5]

Jefferson also saw the ward system as a school and proving ground for future political leaders. Wards would be "the keystone of the arch of our government,"[6] making it possible for America to have a representative federal government that was accountable to a base of active and engaged citizens.

Later in his life, Jefferson moderated his extreme view of rural American virtue, but he continued to give it a central role in the democratic scheme. He realized that a completely agrarian country would breed its own dependency on the manufactured goods of Europe. He later believed that economic independence could be achieved either through land ownership in a rural setting or through achieving a "satisfactory situation" as an urban laborer. But he continued to believe that rural America played a crucial role by maintaining "a due balance between agriculture, manufactures and commerce."[7]

Rural America today

Jefferson never succeeded in amending the Virginia Constitution to adopt the ward system and as America became more urbanized, rural communities played a shrinking role in its political scheme. Dramatic demographic and economic changes in rural America explain much of that shift. By way of illustration, I like to ponder how Jefferson might be surprised if he were to visit the southern West Virginia home where I grew up.

He would see around him vestiges of hillside farms and be shocked to learn that a few hundred feet underneath those hillside farms were catacombs of mine shafts from which coal had been shipped to power plants in Canada and steel mills in Japan. He would learn that the mine three miles away from my house on the north side of the meadow had changed ownership three times in the past fifteen years and had never been owned by a company headquartered closer than Missouri. He would see ridgetops shorn by earth-moving machines taller than the White House. He might speak to a miner and find him tethered to an oxygen tank and hear tales about his fights with Washington bureaucracy over black lung benefits or unemployment checks or enforcement of strip mine laws. With overweight coal trucks barreling down two-lane mountain roads, the rumble of explosives breaking the overburden at a strip mine on the ridge above and the bitter iron-sulfur taste of the well water in his mouth, Jefferson might have felt that living on a hillside farm in southern West Virginia is something like living on the inside of a giant coal-processing factory. He would see in southern West Virginia all of the squalor and dependency that he feared in an urban factory, only magnified many times over because of these communities' physical distance from the actual levers of commercial and political power that must be used to challenge the enterprise.

Of course, southern West Virginia is an extreme example. There are places in rural America today, even in West Virginia, that may boast the economic independence and robust political engagement that Jefferson believed were qualities of rural life. But most of rural America shares the characteristics of southern West Virginia: depopulation, political marginalization and domination by national and multinational corporations.[8]

People and money have shifted away from rural America and with them so has national political power. The last broad social movement based in rural America was the populist movement, which emerged among farmers across the South and Midwest in the 1890s. (The family farm defense movement of the 1980s was much smaller and more localized and did not engage the public imagination to the same extent.) Galvanized in opposition to low prices for produce and the high cost of credit and transportation, the populist movement posed a fundamental and articulate challenge to economic policy, dominated the presidential elections of 1896 and forged temporary alliances with urban workers – but failed to secure the economic changes it sought. The populist movement was the last gasp for the Jeffersonian ideal of rural, agrarian economic independence. Its failure to redress economic policy that favored banks and railroad companies led directly to the crisis of the Great Depression, the depopulation of rural America and the consolidation and industrialization of American agriculture.

A few decades later, the New Deal marked a shift in the role of government, American politics forever changing Jefferson's legacy. Before the New Deal, historians viewed the big story of American history as a struggle between Jeffersonian populists – who fought for broad political participation, decentralized government and decentralized financial institutions – and Hamiltonian federalists, who sought a strong central government and financial institutions. The New Deal scrambled the terms of this equation: President Franklin D. Roosevelt used Hamiltonian means – a strong central government drawing its legitimacy from organized urban unions – in pursuit of egalitarian, participatory, Jeffersonian ends.[9]

The decimation of rural America in the Great Depression, followed by the emergence of a new progressive political structure in the New Deal, sealed the demise of Jefferson's robust vision of the agrarian underpinnings of American democracy. The political foundations of the New Deal were the Democratic political machines of the major cities and predominantly urban labor unions. The rural voice of New Deal progressivism, such as it was, was that of the Dixiecrats. These Southern Democratic political organizations were based with white agricultural landowners who used a reign of terror to keep African-Americans disenfranchised. The Dixiecrats were rural but were eventually discredited by the Civil Rights Movement and they gradually abandoned the New Deal coalition following the passage of the Civil Rights Act of 1964. In the context of these dramatic changes, Jefferson's vision of rural America seemed an anachronism.

Rural organizing today

But the end of the rural idyll of Jefferson's time doesn't mean that rural organizing has no place in modern America. The reasons to organize rural areas today may not be as grand as Jefferson envisioned, but they sprout from the same root.

Sometimes, rural communities are where the action is – at least when it comes to presidential politics. The red and blue electoral college map of the 2004 presidential election reveals that the blue states whose votes went to Democratic Senator John Kerry of Massachusetts are for the most part the urban, coastal states, whereas Republican Texas Governor George Bush won the predominantly rural, red states in the South, West and Midwest. State-level, county-by-county breakdowns show Bush's rural advantage was even more pronounced – Kerry tended to take the urban areas and Bush the suburban and rural ones. In all, Bush won fifty-nine percent of the rural vote.[10]

While America is only twenty-five percent rural, twenty-five percent goes a long way in a tight election. Why did Bush fare so well in rural America? Conventional wisdom suggests that rural Americans supported Bush because they tend toward social conservatism. But in an article that appeared in *The Nation*,[11] reporter John Nichols points out that while rural Americans have always been more socially conservative, at one time they were a reliably Democratic constituency. Rural Americans have fallen away from the Democratic Party, he argues, because it no longer champions the economic issues that are important in rural America.

In his 2004 book *What's the Matter with Kansas*, Thomas Frank shows that rural America has been devastated economically over the past decades. The counties with the highest poverty rates in America are no longer in Appalachia or the Mississippi Delta, but in farming communities on the Great Plains.

Rural America went Republican in 2004, but it isn't reliably so. Neither party has a rural agenda; to both national parties, rural interests are synonymous with agricultural interests as articulated by the national farm lobby, which is dominated by large corporations. Both parties fail to recognize the diversity of issues and livelihoods present in rural America and the common concerns about

education and employment.

The implication of this analysis is that, when it comes to the presidency of the United States, rural America is up for grabs. While social conservatism is important in rural areas, economic issues are more important. The party that develops an agenda that speaks to the livelihood concerns of rural America will carry an important advantage in an important constituency – a shift that will bear national implications.

Constitutional bias

Another reason to organize rural communities is that federal and state constitutions amplify their power. The Constitution gives each state two senators regardless of population – Wyoming's two senators represent 450,000 citizens, while New York's senators represent eighteen million. A double bias favors rural interests in the Electoral College as well. First, each state is allocated votes for each member of Congress, so the Senate bias repeats itself. Second, because of the winner-take-all system, presidential candidates can't afford to campaign only in the most populous states – they must focus on closely-contested states, some of which are rural. Finally, the primary system favors rural states like Iowa and New Hampshire, whose party nomination contests precede those in more urbanized states.

The Constitution was written this way primarily to placate smaller colonies, which feared domination by larger ones. But it is also true that many of the framers were persuaded by Jefferson's view of rural virtue that is inscribed in the document that frames our politics today.

Rural organizing leads to statewide organizing; the two go hand in hand. High incumbency rates among rural state legislators mean they generally occupy important committee positions and therefore will be important to any state legislative strategy. Because rural towns and counties operate with limited budgets, the solution to many rural problems will require action on the state level and therefore a statewide organizing strategy.

When I organized in southern West Virginia, we drove to Charleston to meet with the state highway commissioner to get a two-mile-long gravel road built in Sang Creek Hollow so that kids could ride a bus to school. Stopping coal trucks from barreling down narrow roads in the community of Lake meant getting the director of the state Division of Environmental Protection to meet with two hundred residents in an elementary school cafeteria. It took more meetings with the same director and a meeting with United States Secretary of the Interior Bruce Babbitt arranged through the Citizens Coal Council, to get a coal company to stop blasting rock from a mine site into people's yards.

The county and town governments where these people lived didn't play a big role in the campaigns because they didn't have the money to complete the projects and they didn't have the power to force the coal companies to change. The target of the campaign had to be state government.

Organizers in urban areas, on the other hand, can effect significant change through local governments. In San Antonio, Texas, for example, the San Antonio Communities Organized for Public Service (COPS) and Metro Alliance won

Why Organize Rural America?

millions in the local city budget for after-school programs, job training and living wages for public employees. In the state capital, Austin Interfaith got the local school district to spend over $4 million to build playgrounds at all the city's elementary schools. Such city and county governments administer budgets of hundreds of millions of dollars, operate electric utilities and are the targets of campaigns that affected thousands of families' lives. Of course, these organizations also worked on a statewide agenda in partnership with affiliated Texas organizations and this state-level work aided local initiatives. But local issues did not lead inexorably to state targets as it they often do in rural organizing.

The opposite also is true: statewide organizing leads to rural organizing. Because of incumbency patterns, key legislators tend to be from rural areas. When I worked in Texas, the key committee chairs were from places like Mount Pleasant, San Angelo, Amarillo and Hale Center, but not from Austin, Dallas, or Houston.[12] In West Virginia, key legislative leaders were from Chapmanville and Williamson rather than the Kanawha Valley of Charleston. Rural communities tend to reelect the same people, so rural representatives gain seniority and rise in the ranks of committee hierarchy. Even if economic power lies in the urban centers, political power often literally resides in a small town. To get meetings with those key leaders on important state legislative issues on a reliable basis, you have to have organized constituencies in their districts.

After twenty-five years of organizing primarily in Texas cities, Texas IAF put together the West Texas Organizing Strategy to fill out a statewide organizing strategy and to build leverage with rural West Texas legislators. Even in a predominantly urban state, a statewide organizing strategy cannot be complete without a significant rural component.

Captive polities

Jefferson thought rural America was important to democracy in the nation as a whole because the agrarian life offered economic independence. But today, rural communities often suffer from the worst sort of economic dependence, serving in a colonial capacity as natural resource reservoirs to the national economy. High rates of unemployment and poverty often result. As Jefferson predicted, one result of economic dependency among citizens is that dominant economic interests often capture state political institutions because they can channel money to political campaigns and bring an extraordinary level of resources to bear in a policy dispute. This is one reason why rural communities are unattractive to organize today: even if the people are organized, their power is minor relative to the national or multinational corporations that dominate the state's economy and politics. But that is precisely the reason why it is important to organize a rural state: the nation as a whole suffers if a rural state is captive to the interests of an economically powerful group, because that group's hold on a state gives it disproportionate influence in national elections and policy controversy.

An example of this is the role of the West Virginia vote in the 2000 presidential election. Texas Governor George W. Bush won West Virginia in 2000, the first time a non-incumbent Republican candidate won the state since Theodore Roosevelt was elected president. Had West Virginia voted Democratic, the outcome in Florida would have been irrelevant and Democratic Vice President Al Gore would have won the White House.

The story of how Bush prevailed in a state where Democrats outnumber Republicans two to one was masterfully told in the *Wall Street Journal*.[13] Although coal miners have reliably voted Democratic in presidential elections and Gore won the endorsement of the United Mine Workers of America, he lost the vote of the rank and file because the coal industry lobby successfully portrayed him as favoring enforcement of environmental laws at the expense of coal mining jobs.

Two years earlier, a coalition of environmental organizations filed suit claiming that a coal surface-mining technique called mountaintop removal required creeks to be filled with dirt in violation of the federal Clean Water Act. A Republican-appointed federal judge ruled in their favor and called a halt to all mountaintop mining. Coal mines immediately laid off several thousand miners and claimed the rule meant the end of the mining industry in West Virginia. Afraid of losing their jobs, miners across the state, began picketing the federal courthouse. Ironically, mountaintop removal replaces more labor-intensive deep mining and produces more coal with fewer workers than any other process.[14]

West Virginia's Congressional delegation introduced legislation to amend the provisions of the Clean Water Act that had been violated and the Clinton administration opposed those changes. As the 2000 campaign began, coal industry officials got commitments from Bush to make rule changes to allow mountaintop removal to continue and began to recruit rank-and-file miners to work against Gore. In the end, Bush won with fifty-two percent of the popular vote. Coal companies can now freely fill in creeks and level the tops of mountains and coal employment has continued to fall.

West Virginia is a dramatic illustration of a much broader strategy of the Bush administration to secure Electoral College votes by favoring natural resource industries. The same logic plays out in the states of the Rocky Mountain West.

The coal industry used its power over jobs to influence the presidential choice of its employees, with dramatic impact on the entire nation. (The case could be made that Gore ran a bad campaign in West Virginia and paid the price for taking the miner constituency for granted. Still, the reason the price was paid in this election was because of the way the industry used its power over employment to shape the political debate.) If a state is captive to the interests of an industry and can count on the votes in Congress of its elected representatives, then the national political process is distorted to the detriment of the entire nation.

Today, rural Americans are disproportionately impoverished and unable to act on their interests in the political process. This fact is equally an affront to our democracy and it can only be corrected by organizing rural communities to develop an issue agenda that represents their interests.

Conclusion

Jefferson's enduring insight about American democracy is that for the system to work, its citizens must have a degree of economic independence and participate directly in democratic decision-making at the local level – in schools, labor unions and local government. For him, a certain kind of rural life was a model of this necessary building block for democratic self-governance. Rural America today is a far cry from this model; it is disproportionately poor and dominated by international economic interests. That will only change through political organization and incentives abound to organize rural communities. They have an extra share of power under the Federal Constitution and from higher rates of incumbency. They play a key role in a state organizing strategy. They play a key role in presidential politics. And if we care about democracy, we can't afford to cede any part of our country to corporate interests. For me, the most compelling reason to organize rural is that it simply weakens our commitment to democracy as a people to have anyone, anywhere, unable to use our tools of government to have a say in the basic decisions affecting their lives.

Allen Cooper grew up in Lester, West Virginia. He was founder of the West Virginia Organizing Project and worked for Industrial Areas Foundation projects in Austin and San Antonio, Texas. He holds degrees in law and public policy and currently lives and works in Austin, Texas.

Endnotes

Introduction

[1] The 20 least populated states, in order of most to least populated, are Mississippi, Arkansas, Kansas, Utah, Nevada, New Mexico, West Virginia, Nebraska, Idaho, Maine, New Hampshire, Hawaii, Rhode Island, Montana, Delaware, South Dakota, Alaska, North Dakota, Vermont and Wyoming.

The Country Roads that Created ACORN

[1] The organizers on the drive were Meg Campbell and Stephen Holt.

[2] The organizer on the drive was Stephen Holt.

[3] Steve Kest was ACORN's research director at that time.

[4] This organizing team was led by John Beam.

[5] Bill Kitchen

[6] The editor and author of most of them was Nicholas Lemann, now the head of Columbia School of Journalism and an author and writer for *The New Yorker*.

[7] These were often lightly contested elections, but the fact that we had groups and a deep base in both urban and rural Pulaski County made this possible.

[8] At the time, because of an anomaly in the Arkansas Constitution, we could bill the Quorum Court as one of the "largest legislative bodies in the free world," but immediately after our "takeover" the Constitution was changed by the state legislature to reduce the size to nine members in counties across the state.

[9] Article written by Austin Scott, who had been one of the first African-American Associated Press reporters and was at this time a national reporter for *The Washiongtpn Post*.

[10] Our long-term relationship with the organizations that became WORC – the Western Organization of Resource Councils – and particularly their affiliate the Powder River Basin Resource Council out of Sheridan, Wyoming, was especially helpful in this fight.

[11] Among the great ACORN organizers who worked on these drives were Beth Butler (who left shortly after to run Fort Worth and then Memphis ACORN), Mike Shea (who left to open Denver ACORN) and Mark Shroder (who opened Reno ACORN). Steve Kest came back from college to help at the end and general counsel, Steve Bachmann, ran the legal offense at the PSC. All but one of these folks continues to work with ACORN in one capacity or another now, thirty years later!

Why Organize Rural America?

[1] Charles Louis de Secondat Montesquieu, The Spirit of the Laws.

[2] Federalist 10.

[3] Sheldon, Garrett Ward, *The Political Philosophy of Thomas Jefferson,* Johns Hopkins, Baltimore 1991, p. 76.

[4] Ibid. p. 68

[5] Ibid. p. 70

[6] Ibid. p. 71

[7] Ibid. p. 77

[8] See *Swept Away, Center for Rural Affairs.*

[9] Joseph Ellis, *American Sphinx, Introduction.*

[10] Greenberg, Anna, David Walker and Bill Greener, *"The Message from Rural America: The Rural Vote in 2004,"* from the W.K. Kellogg Foundation, March 22, 2005.

[11] November 2, 2003.

[12] Bill Ratliff, chair of Senate Finance Committee and later Lieutenant Governor, is from Mount Pleasant; Rob Junell, Chair of House Appropriations Committee is from San Angelo, Teal Bivens, Chair of Senate Education Committee, is from Amarillo; and Pete Laney, Speaker of the House, is from Hale Center.

[13] "Bush's Coal Fired Campaign" by Tom Hamburger. June 15, 2001.

[14] Review of how tonnage increased but employment fell as mountaintop removal expanded.